NATURAL
MUSEUMS

NATURAL MUSEUMS

U.S. National Parks, 1872–1916

KATHY S. MASON

Michigan State University Press
East Lansing

∞ The paper used in this publication meets the
minimum requirements of ANSI/NISO Z39.48-1992
(R 1997) (Permanence of Paper).

Michigan State University Press
East Lansing, Michigan 48823-5245

Printed and bound in the United States of America.

10 09 08 07 06 05 04 1 2 3 4 5 6 7 8 9 10

Library of Congress Cataloging-in-Publication Data

Mason, Kathy S., 1970-
    Natural museums: U.S. national parks, 1872–1916 / Kathy S. Mason
        p.   cm.
Includes bibliographical references (p.) and index.
    ISBN 0-87013-711-5 (pbk : alk. paper)
1. National parks and reserves—United States—History
    SB482.A4 M265 2004
    333.78/3/0973 22
2004000270

Michigan State University Press is a member of the
Green Press Initiative and is committed to developing
and encouraging ecologically responsible publishing
practices. For more information about the Green
Press Initiative and the use of recycled paper in book
publishing, please visit www.greenpressinitiative.org.

Cover design by Heidi Dailey
Book design by Bookcomp, Inc.
Cover photograph is of Arch Rock on Mackinac Island
and is used courtesy of Keith Widder

Visit Michigan State University Press on the World Wide Web at:
www.msupress.msu.edu

CONTENTS

Contents

ACKNOWLEGMENTS

I wish to thank Dr. Andrew Cayton, Dr. D. S. Chandler, Dr. David Fahey, Dr. Mary Frederickson, Dr. Adolph Greenberg, and especially my advisor, Dr. Jack Temple Kirby of Miami University for their advice as I developed this project. My fellow graduate students, Michael Clauss, Dr. Paula K. Hinton, and Christina M. Workman, gave constructive criticism of chapter drafts. Dr. Worth Robert Miller, Staci Gates, and Debbie Underwood of Southwest Missouri State University graciously offered their help with some final research.

I am especially grateful to my loved ones. My sister, Dr. Pamela K. Mason, offered her support and advice on the manuscript. Dr. Steven Stannish was always there to lift my spirits. Finally, I would like to express my gratitude to my parents, John S. and Sherri K. Mason, to whom this book is dedicated. Without their encouragement, this endeavor would not have been possible.

INTRODUCTION

Before the National Park Service

In 1872, the U.S. Congress established the world's first national park at Yellowstone. Although notions of nature preservation or conservation were not embraced generally by the American public, five more parks were created before the turn of the century. By 1916, the year that the National Park Service was born, the country could boast fourteen national parks, including such celebrated areas as Yosemite and Sequoia. Although the nation's parks were intended to provide for the "benefit and enjoyment" of all the American people, the parks were concentrated in the sparsely populated western states.

The American public became interested in the parks as vacation destinations in the first decade of the twentieth century; Congressmen also endorsed an increasing number of park proposals. Even with their growing popularity, however, funding, development, and management of the fledgling parks remained as inconsistent as it had been in the nineteenth century. By the 1910s, the Departments of War, Interior, and Agriculture each controlled park units, and all three competed for the meager park appropriations that Congress was willing to provide. Individual park managers struggled to balance the tasks of protecting wildlife and natural "attractions" and providing for the wants and needs of tourists. Without a

single governing body or a general plan for park management, the superintendents had to formulate their own policies for development and protection, often without staffs or the legal machinery needed to enforce
regulations.

The resulting managerial failings and inconsistencies highlighted the
need for a national park service—a bureaucracy that would provide consistent leadership and define park standards. By 1915, the army had become
increasingly weary of its commitment to the national parks. Tensions
between the Department of the Interior and the Department of Agriculture,
stemming from their differing land management philosophies, mounted. In
an attempt to alleviate departmental rivalry and to eliminate some management inconsistencies, Congress created the National Park Service, which
would be controlled by the Department of the Interior.

Although the difficulties of balancing the recreational interests of visitors with notions of nature conservation would continue to plague park
managers throughout the twentieth century, the park service, under the
leadership of Steven T. Mather (from 1917 to 1928), began to set standards
for the national park system that are maintained as ideals today. The significance of Mather's tenure as head of the National Park Service should not be
underestimated. Nonetheless, Congress, park superintendents, and the
American public had formulated general, often tacit, notions concerning the
purpose of the parks long before the park service was created. This book
will explore the origins of national park strategies for recreation, wildlife
protection, and the preservation of natural monuments, and the difficulties
that park managers, federal departments, and eventually the National Park
Service had in implementing them.

In 1872, with the creation of Yellowstone National Park, Congress set a
precedent for the preservation of the monumental, the extraordinary, and
even the bizarre in nature. Early visitors to the parks expected to see grand
natural phenomena that would rival Old World architectural attractions. By
1916, the nation's national parks preserved the world's largest trees, an
amazingly deep lake, an extensive cavern system, and geothermal wonders.

Although Congress was concerned with protecting particular, distinctive
natural attractions, many of its members also wanted to be assured that these
parks would not restrict natural resources valuable to American industry. For
most Americans, the interests of mining, agriculture, and lumbering were

far more important than the protection of scenery. As a consequence, the parks tended to be located on agriculturally marginal lands, particularly in the arid West.

Because the early national parks were designed to protect nature's monuments, wildlife protection was a secondary concern. The late nineteenth-century urban middle class, however, became increasingly interested in the "wilderness" experience that national parks supposedly offered. By 1916, Americans viewed national parks as wilderness and wildlife reserves, as well as tourist attractions. Ironically, roads, concessions, and other facilities that catered to tourists often undermined wildlife protection.

Wilderness preservation has been one of the most problematic national park ideals to implement, because of Americans' ambivalent feelings toward nature, and because "wilderness" has often been difficult to define. Roderick Nash was one of the first historians to examine the wilderness concept in his classic work, *Wilderness and the American Mind*.[1] Offering a comprehensive overview of European Americans' perceptions of the natural world, Nash asserted that the Puritans viewed New England as a desolate, "howling" wilderness that was alien to civilization as they knew it. Thus, from the beginnings of the British colonies, white settlers defined wilderness as the place where civilization, as they knew it, was absent. Native Americans were viewed as part of the wilderness, because they were separated from "civilized" white society.

By the early nineteenth century, a minority of Americans had developed a romantic, aesthetic appreciation of nature. Transcendentalists, such as Henry David Thoreau, celebrated the sublime in nature and argued that contact with wilderness could rejuvenate the soul of the city dweller.[2] John Muir, perhaps America's most celebrated environmental activist of the nineteenth century, embodied the romantic view of nature. Muir championed the cause of wildlife preservation and aesthetic appreciation of wilderness and was the principal defender of Yosemite National Park in the late nineteenth and early twentieth century.

Nash highlights some of the difficulties in protecting national parks and other "wilderness" areas in the twentieth century. Nonetheless, it is often difficult to view national parks as true wilderness when they are crowded with tourists, located in urban areas, feature modern conveniences for visitors, and are managed by human caretakers. Also, Nash fails to ask whether the wilderness ideal taints our relationship with the natural world.

William Cronon has argued that wilderness is an artificial construct, and that Americans celebrate wild lands in an attempt to recapture America's pioneer past. Cronon maintains that the wilderness ideal is dangerous, however, because Americans have begun to view nature as existing only in national parks or wild, remote corners of the globe.[3]

In *Forests: The Shadow of Civilization,* Robert Pogue Harrison maintains that humans' impulse to exist apart from the wilderness is not a new phenomenon. The Western world traditionally has used forests to "mark the provincial edge of Western civilization, in the literal as well as imaginative domains." Civilization and wilderness are defined against each other; the loss of wilderness, whether real or perceived, thus creates anxiety in the Western mind, for the concept of civilization ceases to be meaningful.[4] Americans may have a deep need for their national parks to be seen as "wilderness" areas, whether or not these areas are crowded or overdeveloped.

Because national parks were supposed to be tourist attractions, wildlife preserves, and symbols of American greatness, every park should have been significant for the country as a whole. Nonetheless, a number of national parks (most notably, Platt) seemed to attract mostly local visitors. Although the majority of the national parks were not easily accessible to easterners, a park's national importance became critical if its worthiness as a monument or preserve were ever called into question. Even park boosters attacked Wind Cave, Sully's Hill, and Hot Springs because they did not meet the standard for beauty set by Yosemite and other park "gems," and thus devalued the system as a whole. Park historian Duane Hampton has argued that even National Park Service employees have attacked "inferior" parks, because these units siphon scarce funding away from more popular, "worthy" areas.[5] The parks' national significance, monumentalism, tourism, wilderness character, and economic worthlessness, therefore, are all considered in this study.

Although much has been written about the U.S. national parks, surprisingly few professional historians have examined their early history. The bulk of national park literature consists of guidebooks and the travel logs and memoirs of explorers and park employees. A few laudatory (although not wholly uncritical) studies of the park system have been written by Interior Department employees and park boosters as well.

Nevertheless, the number of scholarly treatments of park history is growing with the increasing popularity of environmental history. Alfred Runte was probably the most important U.S. national park historian to emerge in the late twentieth century. The originator of the "worthless lands thesis" in 1973, Runte argued that the national parks initially were intended to protect nothing but monumental scenery, and that the nation has been unwilling to protect lands that might have value to lumbering, mining, or agricultural interests.[6]

There are other useful secondary sources for national park history. John Ise's massive *Our National Park Policy* (1961) details the legislative and administrative history of the national parks, although it glosses over the complexities of balancing conservation, recreation, and preservation ideals.[7] Duane Hampton's laudatory *How the U.S. Cavalry Saved Our National Parks* (1971) is also one of the few works to examine the army's role in early national park history.[8] In spite of some shortcomings, these works, along with park superintendents' reports, congressional and departmental records, park guidebooks, and travel literature, provide important sources for this book.

By examining individual parks, this book traces the development of park ideas and management standards before 1916. It demonstrates how these general notions were used to evaluate particular parks, shows the unique management problems that some parks presented, and addresses the differences between civilian and army park supervision. Lesser-known parks and units that are no longer included in the national park system are also featured prominently in this work. An examination of these supposedly inferior areas, which are usually ignored by historians, highlights what Congress and the public deemed worthy of preservation and what steps managers were willing to take to ensure a park's status.

The first chapter examines the precursor of the national parks—Hot Springs Reservation in Arkansas. This reserve set a precedent for the protection of natural recreation areas. Chapter two turns to the world's first national park—Yellowstone. The importance of monumentalism and industrial "worthlessness" in the creation of this park is emphasized, as well as the management and funding difficulties that resulted in an army administration for the park.

The army's role as park protector at Mackinac, Sequoia, General Grant, and Yosemite National Parks is also examined in chapters three and four. Mackinac National Park, which has been neglected by most park literature, is an especially interesting case. Unlike the earliest western parks, it drew large numbers of tourists and served as both a historical and a natural attraction. Nonetheless, Mackinac's superintendent had to face the typical challenge of balancing the protection of natural scenery with the recreational interests of visitors, often with little federal funding.

Chapter five examines three less famous parks—Wind Cave in South Dakota, Sullys Hill in North Dakota, and Platt in Oklahoma. Soon after they received national park status, these parks were labeled "inferior" by the secretary of the interior and by many park writers. Nonetheless, the Interior Department (which controlled these parks) and individual superintendents attempted to improve the parks' wildlife and recreational attractions, thereby making the reserves "worthy" of their status. For Wind Cave and Sullys Hill, this meant the addition of wildlife preserves, which would be maintained by the Department of Agriculture.

The final chapter examines the creation of the National Park Service. The army's rejection of its role as park protector and the conflicting land management philosophies of the Agriculture and the Interior Departments are discussed. The roots of the park system's standards were established long before Steven Mather took charge of the new National Park Service.

Thus, by examining the parks in the order that they were founded, I hope to demonstrate the evolution of park concepts, including those of monumentalism, wildlife protection, and public recreation. This approach also will highlight the unique challenges that each park presented—especially before a single agency controlled all of the parks. Although most environmental historians choose to focus on the famous national park "gems," the histories of Mackinac, Sully's Hill, and other less-known parks underscore both the fragility of the early parks' status and a lack of formal national park standards. When a park became too inconvenient to manage or fund, when it was seen as valuable to industry, or when it could not boast a grand natural monument or curiosity, the park's status was called into question. I contend that an examination of supposedly "inferior" parks is as important to our understanding of the early history of America's parks as is a study of Yellowstone, Yosemite, and other "crown jewel" parks.

ONE

Origins of an Idea

Hot Springs Reservation

Although Yellowstone became the first national reserve to bear the designation "national park," Arkansas Hot Springs was the first attempt by the United States to preserve a natural resource for the public's use. Established in 1832, the Hot Springs Reservation placed forty-seven springs in central Arkansas under federal jurisdiction. Because the reservation did not possess the grand scenery or monumental attractions of Yosemite, Yellowstone, or Sequoia, America's earliest experiment in nature conservation has been largely ignored by park boosters and historians.[1] Nonetheless, as America's nineteenth-century national parks were created for "the benefit and enjoyment" of the general public, so, too, did the Hot Springs Reservation develop into a resort that catered to the health and recreational needs of its visitors.

Even though the federally controlled reserve at Arkansas Hot Springs was unique in the early nineteenth century, its creation was inspired by the longstanding traditions of public, urban parks and royal forests in Europe. Many Americans were interested in the hot springs because mineral springs bathing was a time-honored treatment for illness and injury in Europe. In addition, the Hot Springs Reserve demonstrates how spas of the nineteenth century developed from being treatment centers for invalids to being fashionable resorts for the middle and upper classes. Finally, the federal government hoped that by controlling the healing waters of this developing health resort, the United States would avoid European criticism of American tastes. Specifically, Congress hoped to avoid the kind of national embarrassment that resulted from the environmental degradation and commercial development around Niagara Falls, America's most famous natural tourist attraction in the early nineteenth century.

The hot springs that attracted the attention of the U.S. government in the early nineteenth century are located in the Ouachita Mountains of Arkansas. The springs produce slightly less than one million gallons of water per day, with the temperature of some of the springs reaching more than 140 degrees Farenheit. The mountains are heavily wooded and are popular with present-day hikers.

Native Americans utilized the hot springs for centuries. Prehistoric peoples probably quarried novaculite in the area.[2] Many Indian tribes, including the Caddos, Choctaws, Cherokees, and Quapaws, settled in central Arkansas in the eighteenth and nineteenth centuries. The hot springs were a popular place to rest and recover from injuries or ailments. The Indians built no bathing facilities around the springs, choosing instead to sit or lie in natural pools or spring-carved channels. White Americans most closely associated the Quapaws with the springs, because that tribe's members were placed on a reservation in the area in the early nineteenth century. By 1818, however, the federal government had removed the Quapaws to present-day Oklahoma.[3]

The first Europeans to visit the springs were probably Hernando de Soto's troops. Members of de Soto's army reported that in September and October, 1541, they had visited hot springs and had watered their horses at warm, brackish pools near the Ouachita river. Although nineteenth-century promoters of Hot Springs claimed imaginatively that de Soto and his men had found their "fountain of youth," de Soto himself did not live long after he left the supposedly healing, restorative waters of Arkansas.[4]

By the turn of the eighteenth century, a small stream of white visitors from the southern United States and the New Orleans area frequented the Arkansas Hot Springs during the summer months, hoping to alleviate their arthritis pain or to regain their strength after extended illnesses. After the purchase of the Louisiana Territory in 1803, Thomas Jefferson proposed an expedition into the region between the Red and Arkansas Rivers. Jefferson apparently had heard reports of hot springs in the area and was interested in their scientific and medical value. Jefferson appointed his friend, William Dunbar, and Dr. George Hunter to lead the expedition.

With a small military escort, the Hunter-Dunbar expedition left Natchez in October 1804. The party traveled up the Red River to the Black, and finally up the Ouachita. When the expedition arrived at the springs in December, Hunter and Dunbar found a small collection of crude shacks and huts that white visitors had built over the springs to protect themselves from the elements as they bathed. Dunbar and Hunter later reported that the springs had a reputation for providing great relief from rheumatism and joint pain.[5]

During the next two decades, the springs continued to entertain a steady stream of visitors who came to restore their health. A few enterprising individuals built small rental cabins, while others made money by providing food for visitors. By the 1820s, doctors had established summertime practices at the springs, advising patients on the proper use of the waters. During the 1820s and early 1830s, small hotels were built and the first bathhouses, featuring wooden tubs, were constructed to accommodate visitors. Hundreds of people were traveling to the springs every summer.

John Pope, the territorial governor of Arkansas, saw both the springs' potential health benefits and the prestige that a resort could bring to the area, and lobbied the federal government to build a public bathing facility in the developing town of Hot Springs. Although Congress did not act on this proposal, it was willing to prevent the private "appropriation" of the springs. On 20 April 1832, Congress passed the resolution that "set apart" the springs and "the four sections of land" surrounding it. Thus, the Hot Springs Reserve was born.[6]

Although Hot Springs was a forerunner to the world's first national park at Yellowstone, public parks and protected areas were not alien to America or Europe. Royal forests and hunting grounds had existed in Europe since the Middle Ages. Commons and gardens were protected places used by the general public. By the nineteenth century, most European towns and cities could boast of an urban park or "public walk" where residents could stroll and socialize. Such parks were a source of civic pride and were intended to provide wholesome recreational opportunities for the general public.[7] Community walks and parks also provided refuge for residents of rapidly expanding, increasingly industrial European cities.

Keeping this tradition, the United States founded its earliest parks and reserves, in part, as recreation areas and escapes from hectic urban life. The most prominent U.S. example of a constructed, urban park in the nineteenth century was New York City's Central Park. Designed by America's premiere landscape architect, Frederick Law Olmsted, this artfully designed green space was a recreational oasis for harried residents who wanted to retreat from the noise and bustle of the city.[8]

Even though the Hot Springs Reserve's roots could be traced to Old World traditions, Congress's decision to establish the reserve was also influenced by the intense commercial development around Niagara Falls. In the early and mid-nineteenth century, Niagara Falls was probably North America's most famous natural attraction and one of its most popular tourist destinations. Nevertheless, tacky souvenir shops, seedy tourist hotels, scenic overlooks that charged visitors for a glimpse of the natural wonder, and colored lights projected onto the falls at night were a keen source of embarrassment for both the U.S. and Canadian governments. Visitors also had to contend with factories and other unsightly industrial structures when they came to enjoy the aesthetic merits of the falls. For many visitors, the view was made even less impressive by mills and other industrial enterprises that diverted water and diminished the flow over the falls. While the U.S. government generally valued industry over nature preservation, it was unwilling leave Hot Springs at the mercy of crass developers and hucksters.[9]

Americans' general interest in health resorts and hot springs bathing could be linked to their longing for European refinement. European spas such as Bath, Baden-Baden, and Carlsbad, which had been retreats for the sick for centuries, became vacation destinations for the wealthy by the nineteenth century. America had its own versions of these fashionable resorts in the early 1800s. Saratoga, Newport, and French Lick, Indiana, evolved from quiet, undeveloped havens for invalids into major social centers. Foster Rhea Dulles, historian of American recreation, noted that visits to such spas became critical to maintaining one's place in polite society in the mid-nineteenth century.[10]

Thus, the long tradition of spring bathing for medical purposes, combined with America's cultural insecurity, led to the establishment of Hot Springs Reserve. Hot Springs, however, was not immediately hailed as one of America's premiere resorts. Although its Arkansas location made Hot Springs an attractive destination for southerners, America's most famous and fashionable resorts, such as Saratoga in New York, were in the north.[11] Travel to Hot Springs in the first half of the nineteenth century was also arduous, especially for visitors who were seriously ill. Most traveled by steamboat from New Orleans to Little Rock, and then took a hack or stagecoach to the springs. Some visitors took rude trails directly from the Mississippi. The Ouachita Mountains, which are considered picturesque by modern tourists and hikers, made travel by stage exceedingly difficult, with the trip from Little Rock taking a day and a half.[12]

Although the resort's most frail patients endured a great deal of discomfort during travel, an unlimited supply of hot water for bathing must have been a supreme luxury for nineteenth-century Americans.[13] This, combined with vague testimonials as to the healing power of the minerals in the springs, attracted new pilgrims with each passing year.

Hot Springs became a virtual ghost town during the Civil War. The number of summertime bathers, however, increased immediately after the hostilities ended. By this time, doctors had permanent practices at the springs, although many visitors chose not to consult them. While bathing rituals varied, depending on the policies of the bathhouses and hotels, the advice of physicians, or the preferences of the bathers, Hot Springs guests usually soaked in spring-fed tubs, sat in steam baths, or drank hot spring water in order to cleanse the body from the inside out. Although the bathhouses provided formal bathing rituals, complete with modern equipment (such as porcelain tubs) and bath attendants, many bathers chose to use open-air, spring-fed pools. One of the most popular in the 1870s was the Ral Hole. Bathers would soak in the pool or cover themselves with mud from the bank and lie in the sun. Female bathers used the pool in the morning, while the men claimed it in the afternoon.[14]

The number of visitors increased substantially when the railroad extended to the growing town of Hot Springs in 1875. Hot Springs, however, had architectural and environmental problems that undermined the spa image that local business owners wished to cultivate. Most of the hotels were still modest, two-story structures. Furthermore, unsanitary conditions rose in town as visitation and development increased. The most visible threat to public health was the Hot Springs Creek, which had become a virtual sewer and hog wallow even though it ran through the center of town.[15]

Until the 1870s, the federal government showed very little concern for the management of the springs or the regulation of bathing practices there. In 1877, however, Benjamin F. Kelley was appointed the first superintendent of the reserve. His and his successors' duties included setting and collecting fees from the hotels and bathhouses for use of the water, evicting squatters from the reserve, and providing baths for the poor.[16] In the final two decades of the nineteenth century, the city of Hot Springs underwent a number of substantive changes. Most significantly, an archway and a paved road were built over the Hot Springs Creek, creating the resort's famous promenade. A federally controlled veteran's hospital was also constructed.

The most significant development in Hot Springs at the turn of the century, however, was the construction of increasingly luxurious bathing facilities along the promenade. The architecture of the new hotels and bathhouses was strikingly eclectic and anachronistic. Renaissance Spanish, French, Mediterranean, and even Byzantine styles were employed. The owners hoped that such facades would convey an air of European elegance; a modern-day writer labeled it a nineteenth-century Las Vegas.[17] These co-opted Old World architectural styles, however, were a hallmark of the area's twentieth-century tourism, and brought ever-increasing numbers of visitors to town, including gangsters such as Al Capone. The gambling that these disreputable vacationers brought to town undermined the elegant spa image that hotel and bathhouse owners wished to cultivate.

Obviously, Hot Springs bathhouse developers were not concerned with creating a unique architectural style that would be more appropriate for the area. Furthermore, very few of the resort's early boosters showed any interest in promoting the natural surroundings as a means of attracting tourists. Early-nineteenth-century visitors to Hot Springs were concerned with recovering their health, rather than contemplating the aesthetic merits of the Ouachita Mountains. As travel to the springs became easier, however, visitors and promoters were far more likely to appreciate the area's natural beauty. Nonetheless, the bathing facilities and the springs that fed them were the primary concerns of the reserve's superintendent. In the late nineteenth century, all of the major springs in town were capped, in part to prevent pollution, but also to better regulate water distribution to bathhouses and hotels. Ironically, promoters sang the praises of the "Valley of the Vapors" even as the clouds of steam that had shrouded the mountains were reduced by the capping.[18]

The federal government's lack of interest in the area's natural surroundings is striking, considering that the earliest national parks, such as Yellowstone and Yosemite, preserved monumental natural attractions. Both the Hot Springs Reserve and the early parks, however, provided recreational opportunities for their visitors. Also, neither Hot Springs nor the other early national parks were intended to preserve wilderness. Hot Springs protected a resource that provided for the public's health and welfare, while Yellowstone and other nineteenth-century parks were meant to preserve exotic or remarkable natural phenomena. Wild lands protection initially was a by-product. If anything, the earliest visitors to Hot Springs, who had to travel by stagecoach, viewed Arkansas's wild lands as a nuisance. Only when Hot Springs became more urbanized and travel became easier did visitors begin to appreciate the area's natural beauty.

The long history of Hot Springs as a spa, however, did appeal to romantics. Nineteenth- and early-twentieth-century promoters of the U.S. reserve often invoked Native Americans' past use of the springs, or the Spanish "discovery" of the area, in promotional literature. Of course, it was relatively simple for writers to create sentimental, romantic tales of Native American life in the area after the original inhabitants had been removed. One advertising pamphlet from the early twentieth century claimed that the springs' "clouds of healing vapors . . . struck the primitive Indians with awe and they believed that the Great Spirit abode [sic] in them. . . . [A] peace pact was made, leaving the miraculous waters to the Great Spirit's own control." With claims that individuals from all tribes were "made whole" by the springs, the pamphleteer assured the reader that hot springs therapy offered mysterious, time-honored, and virtually miraculous results.[19]

Indeed, most authors of tourist guides and promotional literature emphasized the area's antiquity. One hyperbolic tourist guide stated:

long before Cortez frightened the Aztecs, . . .
long before Columbus ruddered his way to America;
yea, while the Crusaders were marching toward
the holy Tomb, ah, before the mud wall of the
village of Rome was dry, the North American
Indians traveled hundreds of miles to Hot
Springs, the fountain of youth, to sit in wise council and to regain
their health.[20]

Although the author invoked Native Americans' past use of the springs to attract white middle- and upper-class tourists, he also stated reassuringly that "(t)here is no rawness" at Hot Springs, because "all has been mellowed by time." Even though "simple children of nature" had benefited from the springs in the past, modern visitors would not find primitive accommodations there now.[21] Of course, this meant that they would not find Native Americans either.

Embellished tales of the Spanish arrival at the springs were also staples of travel guides. Not surprisingly, stories of the Spaniards' discovery of the waters' wondrous powers were retold with such frequency that writers often confused de Soto and his quest for gold with Ponce de Leon and his quest for the fountain of youth.[22]

With the growing emphasis on opulent accommodations, the resort's medical functions could be easily overlooked. Hot Springs, however, still cared for the desperately ill, as well as the pleasure seekers. The early reputation of

Hot Springs as a health spa was based upon the relief the waters supposedly provided to rheumatics; by the turn of the century, however, the majority of patients seeking treatment at the springs were suffering from sexually trans-mitted diseases—particularly syphilis. Before the development of antibi-otics, the preferred treatment for syphilis was mercury. Treatment of the disease at Hot Springs varied from standard practice because it used as much as ten times the amount of mercury that was normally recommended and it was accompanied by a doctor-prescribed regimen of baths. The mercury was either applied directly to the skin, or the patient sat in a mercury vapor bath.[23]

Of course, such treatments were largely ineffectual. Health profession-als could not agree on a proper dosage of mercury to effect a cure, and large doses of the substance could cause serious skeletal and neurological dam-age. Also, many patients assumed that they were cured of syphilis, only to have their symptoms reoccur after they left the springs. Federal health inspectors occasionally found unsanitary conditions in bathhouses and hotels, such as patients drinking from the same water glass or tubs that were not cleaned properly.

In spite of this, Hot Springs remained a popular treatment center because of the accommodations and the mysterious healing properties of the springs. Nineteenth-century visitors believed that the waters' healing powers were linked to its mineral content. In the early twentieth century, however, the springs were thought to be slightly radioactive, which was sup-posed to enhance the body's ability to resist disease. In fact, the springs are not radioactive, but Hot Springs boosters, as well as more levelheaded national park critics, viewed the radioactive waters as an important resource that needed to be preserved for the American public.[24]

The superintendent of Hot Springs Reserve was partially responsible for maintaining the town's reputation as a health spa. At the end of the nine-teenth century, Superintendent William J. Little monitored the springs' min-eral content, regulated the fees that bathhouses charged their clients, kept track of the amount of spring water that bathing facilities used, and attempted to circumscribe the influence that unlicensed doctors and other medical quacks had over visitors. Reserve regulations prohibited hotels and baths from "drumming" up clients with outrageous medical claims or offers of free baths. Superintendent Little believed that such practices could harm patients and undermine the reserve's image.[25]

When the U.S. National Park Service was created in 1916, Hot Springs Reserve was placed under the protection of the new agency. Steven Mather, the first director of the National Park Service, campaigned strongly for Hot

Springs to be designated a national park. Hot Springs was the most frequently visited park service unit, and Mather believed that the creation of a
national park at the springs would boost public support for the service. In
1921, Congress granted Mather's wish and Hot Springs Reserve became Hot
Springs National Park.[26]

Robert Sterling Yard, a former assistant of Steven Mather and one of the
National Park Service's most ardent supporters, did not agree with Mather's
policy of granting park status to popular regional attractions. In 1919, with
Mather's blessing, Yard had become the first president of the National Parks
Association, a nonpartisan group dedicated to the defense of the national
parks. Yard argued that reserves like Hot Springs, which had regional appeal
and pleasant scenic attributes, would undermine the reputation of the
whole national park system because they did not possess the superlative
natural beauty, grandeur, or unique monumental features that characterized
Yellowstone, Yosemite, and other early national parks.[27] Nonetheless, Hot
Springs National Park did indeed have public appeal, and it did serve a
recreational function for its visitors.

The widespread use of antibiotics to treat disease sounded the death
knell for the medicinal use of the springs. After World War II, the springs'
popularity tapered off, and all but one of the bathhouses, the Buckstaff,
closed. Today, the National Park Service emphasizes the scenic hiking trails
of the Ouachita Mountains and the history of the area's bathing industry.
The national park's visitor center is located in the old Fordyce Bathhouse.
Built in 1915, it was probably the town's most elegant and modern bathhouse, with a gymnasium, an indoor pool, and large hubbard tubs, which
were designed for patients suffering from paralysis.[28] Modern visitors still
enjoy baths at Hot Springs hotels and bathhouses—but for relaxation and
analgesic purposes only, not for the cure of ailments.

Thus, America's first experiment with land conservation was a highly developed, highly utilized health spa. Even though such national reserves
(including the national parks) were American inventions, the underlying
ideals were rooted in Old World urban park traditions. The earliest reservation in the United States had none of the monumental attractions or sublime scenery associated with the other early parks; it simply preserved a
natural resource for visitors to enjoy. Hot Springs was not intended to be a
wilderness preserve, though it did establish the precedent of national reserves serving as recreation areas.

By setting aside the medicinal waters, Congress hoped that Hot Springs would develop into a genteel and elegant resort. Obviously, the results were mixed. While the federal government regulated water purity and the quality of bathing facilities, bathhouse architecture, quack physicians, and local amusements (which were beyond federal control) undermined the resort's spa image. Interestingly, the water of Hot Springs is still a popular drink with tourists—not for its mineral content or radioactive properties, but because of its purity.[29] Even today, the waters seem to possess a rare and valuable quality.

TWO

A Worthless Wonderland
Yellowstone National Park

Although the Hot Springs Reservation and Yosemite Park were the nation's first attempts to reserve lands for recreational, scientific, and aesthetic purposes, Yellowstone became the world's first true "national park" in 1872. Historian Alfred Runte has argued that Yellowstone was granted the title "national park" because Wyoming was still a territory, and, as a result, the federal government retained ownership of the park lands.[1] While Yellowstone's new title may not have had any particular importance at the time, the park possessed the unique natural curiosities and monumental attractions that Americans ultimately came to expect in every national park. According to John Ise, it was almost a "miracle" that Congress was willing to grant Yellowstone park status.[2] Americans generally valued nature for its utility for logging, grazing, farming, or mining enterprises; only a few romantics embraced aesthetic conservation. Yellowstone's supporters, however, were able to convince Congress that the future park was worthless to industry and agriculture.

Although Yellowstone's geysers and hot springs were initially reserved as scientific wonders and points-of-interest for sightseers, the park itself quickly became a big game preserve that would protect buffalo and elk as symbols of America's vanishing frontier heritage. Of course, Yellowstone's earliest managers had no experience in balancing the interests of tourists and concessionaires with wildlife protection. This dilemma continues to plague park superintendents today.

Yellowstone National Park's primary function, however, was to preserve extraordinary landscapes that would edify the American public. Such monumental scenery made it one of the "crown jewels" of the park system.[3] Monumentalism thus was the first major criterion for national park status.

Yellowstone's beauty and striking natural curiosities were celebrated decades before it became a national park. John Colter, a fur trapper who had been a member of the Lewis and Clark Expedition, is believed to have been the first white man to view the region. Other trappers, such as Jim Bridger, brought fantastic tales of Yellowstone's natural wonders to the East. Most of Bridger's audience viewed his stories with a great deal of skepticism, for he was notorious for his exaggerations and lies. Indeed, while Bridger's tales of boiling pools of mud and steaming water shooting from the ground would have engendered skepticism from any audience, his descriptions of petrified birds singing petrified songs cemented his reputation as a teller of tall tales.[4]

For most nineteenth-century Americans, an accurate description of Yellowstone's wonders would have been too fantastic to believe. Thermal geysers, terraced hot springs, and a waterfall that was twice as high as Niagara Falls were difficult for most Americans, especially easterners, to imagine. Thus, extraordinary sites such as Old Faithful, Mammoth Hot Springs, and the Lower Falls of the Yellowstone River became major attractions in the future national park.

Rumors of Yellowstone's extraordinary natural curiosities continued to circulate decades after Colter "discovered" Yellowstone. In 1870, a group of Helena, Montana's most prominent men decided to explore the region and view these fabled wonders for themselves. The expedition was led by General Henry D. Washburn, surveyor general of Montana and a former U.S. congressman, and Nathaniel P. Langford, collector of internal revenue for Montana.

This expedition was endorsed wholeheartedly by Lieutenant General Philip Sheridan. Sheridan had taken a keen interest in the area after hearing fantastic tales of Yellowstone's geysers and hot springs during an inspection tour of Montana's forts.[5] Therefore, he authorized a military escort, led by Lieutenant Gustavus C. Doane, to accompany the civilian party. Langford,

Doane, and other members of the Washburn Expedition would eventually champion the cause of Yellowstone National Park.

During their month-long tour of the area, the members of the expedition viewed many of Yellowstone's most famous sites. Near the end of the excursion, the party expressed enthusiasm for the establishment of a public park in the area. Nathaniel Langford credited Judge Cornelius Hedges with proposing the idea. In any case, Hedges and Langford became the park concept's most ardent advocates. Hedges's account of the party's adventure was printed in the *Helena Herald* soon after the group's return, and the expedition's adventures were reported in major newspapers across the country.[6] Early in 1871, Langford delivered lectures in support of the park concept in Washington and New York. Truman C. Everts's sensational description of his "Thirty-Seven Days of Peril" after his separation from the rest of the Washburn-Doane party was printed in *Scribner's Magazine* in November 1871.[7]

The publicity that the Washburn-Doane party generated for Yellowstone did not pass unnoticed in Washington. In the summer of 1871, the U.S. Geological and Geographical Survey of the Territories sent a party of scientists, photographer William Jackson, and artist Thomas Moran to explore the area. The group's leader, Dr. Ferdinand V. Hayden, became a champion of the park concept. His testimony before the House Committee on the Public Lands convinced many congressmen that Yellowstone would make an appropriate park for the nation.

The proponents of the Yellowstone National Park idea found two allies in Congress. During the second session of the forty-second Congress, William H. Clagett, the delegate from Montana, and Senator Samuel Pomeroy from Kansas introduced legislation that would set aside 2.3 million acres of Wyoming, Montana, and Idaho land as Yellowstone National Park.[8] Pomeroy's and Hayden's statements attesting to the virtual worthlessness of the land for productive enterprises, save geologic research, garnered much support for the measure.

The park bill, however, did have detractors. Senator Cornelius Cole of California was not convinced that the land was completely worthless for cultivation. He also stated that the geysers and natural curiosities would remain, "no matter where the ownership of the land may be." Cole did not simply believe that settlement and agriculture took precedence over a public park; he assumed that these lands would not require government protection in the first place if they were indeed as worthless as their supporters claimed.[9]

In spite of Cole's objections, most senators favored the bill. Senator Lyman Trumbull of Illinois argued that any individual could "plant himself right across the only path" if Congress did not protect Yellowstone.[10]

Although most senators would have questioned the park proposal if Hayden had not been so forceful in asserting that Yellowstone was worthless to agriculture and industry, they were unwilling to allow Yellowstone's wonders to be exploited by a single concessionaire.

Cultural insecurity also was a major factor in the creation of Yellowstone National Park, as it had been when Congress established the Hot Springs Reserve. Many American intellectuals and political leaders were sensitive to European criticisms of American tastes and culture. In particular, American architecture seemed to pale in comparison to Europe's. A tour of Europe was thus a requirement for any American with money and pretensions of refinement. Although America's museums and churches did not measure up to Europe's in the nineteenth century, Yellowstone's natural wonders and "adornments" potentially eclipsed anything Europe could offer. Hayden, who was keenly interested in self-promotion, became an ardent advocate for a park that would become a testament to the grandeur of the United States. Yellowstone's ability to inspire feelings of national pride contributed significantly to the creation of the park.[11]

The park bill also was attractive to Congress because the creation of the reserve would cost the government nothing. In his attempts to ensure the passage of the measure, Hayden intimated that the park could be self-supporting through tourist concessions.[12] The park's supporters correctly assumed that the measure would garner more votes if the park appeared to be self-sustaining. Congress also was unwilling to let sentiment get in the way of productive enterprise. Senator Trumbull and Representative Henry L. Dawes of Massachusetts, who had supported the park idea, pointed out that the park act could be rescinded at any time if the land was found to possess any value other than scenery.[13]

In the end, the House passed the Senate's version of the Yellowstone National Park Bill. On 1 March 1872, President Grant signed the act that set aside more than two million acres as "a park or pleasuring ground for the benefit and enjoyment of the people." The new park would be under the "exclusive control" of the Department of the Interior. This experiment in land preservation was not as progressive as it could have been, however, because Congress reserved the right to rescind the park act at any time. Nathaniel Langford, as the park's superintendent, was expected to protect the park's curiosities and provide for the safety and comfort of visitors with no financial support from the federal government.

There were difficulties with the Yellowstone National Park Act itself that would hamper the superintendent's effectiveness in managing the park. While the act stated the purpose of the park's creation, it made no legal provisions for the park. Furthermore, it did not provide penalties for infractions committed within the park. Hiram Chittenden, Yellowstone's first major historian, viewed this omission as the greatest obstacle to effective management in the park's early years.[14] The chronic lack of federal funds and legal machinery would be obstacles that the early civilian superintendents of Yellowstone could not overcome.

Because of his great love for Yellowstone and his tremendous enthusiasm for the national park idea, Nathaniel Langford was a natural choice for the first park superintendent's position. Unfortunately, his five years as superintendent of Yellowstone National Park proved to be disheartening for the man who had earned the nickname "National Park" Langford.[15] Langford received no salary or operating funds from the federal government. He also had no staff to aid him in his duties. His appeals for funds and judicial machinery to enforce regulations fell on deaf ears in Washington. Langford spent most of his tenure as park superintendent in Minnesota, where he earned his living as a bank examiner. During his administration, he was vilified in western papers for his ineffectual leadership in developing and protecting the park.

Fortunately for both Langford's reputation and the park's integrity, few tourists visited Yellowstone immediately after its establishment. Indeed, the tiny Hot Springs Reservation was a greater tourist attraction.[16] Langford's successors to the position of park superintendent would not be as lucky. As tourism in Yellowstone increased, so too did the number of administrative headaches for the park superintendents.

Although trips to Europe and relaxing visits to spas were the preferred vacations for middle- and upper-class Americans in the late nineteenth century, easterners began about this time to take an interest in the West. Many of Yellowstone National Park's earliest visitors, however, came to "sightsee," rather than to have a rugged camping experience. As Roderick Nash has noted, Yellowstone's earliest supporters were not interested in wilderness preservation. Instead, they were concerned with protecting points-of-interest that would edify the visitor and testify to America's greatness. Yellowstone's early role in "wilderness" protection was unintentional.[17]

Sightseeing tours did not necessarily generate appreciation for Yellowstone, because the park's wonders seemed so exceedingly bizarre that they occasionally repelled as well as impressed visitors. One traveler reflected this ambivalence as he described Yellowstone as "overburdened with strange creations that have no counterpart anywhere in the world." He also hailed the park as "a strange, weird storehouse of natural wonders." In *American Notes,* Rudyard Kipling described a portion of Yellowstone as "blistered, peeled and abominable, and given over to the sporting and spouting of devils who threw mud, and steam, and dirt at each other with whoops." When he looked down a geyser cone, he "beheld a horrible, slippery, slimy funnel." Kipling, however, was impressed with the park and lamented the vandalism committed by "irreverent Americans." In any case, most vacationers wanted to see impressive natural monuments, not untamed wild lands.[18] Nature conservation was of secondary importance, and the demands that visitors placed upon the park jeopardized wildlife as well as the attractions that tourists came to see.

Vandalism became a major problem in Yellowstone Park as the number of visitors increased. Many Yellowstone visitors were not above obtaining souvenirs from notable rock formations, throwing debris into springs, carving their names into popular natural attractions, or even attempting to destroy geyser cones. Careless tourists also threatened acres of timber by leaving their campfires unattended.

Even when Congress finally granted appropriations to the park superintendent in 1878, there was little he could do to stop such depredations. Although Yellowstone's second superintendent, Philetus W. Norris, had more success in developing the park than did N. P. Langford, his road-building projects did not offer protection to the park's natural attractions. Indeed, such projects probably gave vandals greater access to these sites.[19]

In 1883, Congress finally granted the funds necessary to hire ten assistant superintendents to aid the superintendent in protecting the park. The secretary of the interior was charged with making these appointments. Unfortunately, this new ranger force was not effective in protecting the park. The assistant superintendents were political appointees with few management skills and little experience with the outdoors. Even when these men were conscientious in their duties, they were virtually powerless to enforce park regulations because the only legal recourse at their disposal was to expel the violator.[20]

Vandalism was not the only human threat to the park. Poaching was also a violation of the national park act, which prohibited the wanton destruction of game and wildlife in Yellowstone. Lieutenant General Philip Sheridan took issue with the seemingly unchecked slaughter of the park's animals by hunters and tourists during his second tour of Yellowstone in 1882. Sheridan insisted that the army could offer better protection for the park than the Department of Interior ever could, and could make Yellowstone a "place of refuge and safety for our noble game."[21] Furthermore, Sheridan argued that it would be far more economical for the park to be protected by troops.[22] In the past, Sheridan had had few reservations concerning the killing of buffalo, for the slaughter of these animals had simultaneously weakened Native American tribes. Apparently, Sheridan had by this point rethought his position on the destruction of buffalo, now that Native Americans posed little threat to the advancement of white civilization in the West and the buffalo were in danger of becoming extinct.

Sheridan probably assumed that Yellowstone could now be a perfect game refuge because Superintendent Norris had assured the public that there was no significant Indian presence in the Yellowstone area. With Custer's debacle at Little Big Horn in the not-so-distant past, Norris wanted to reassure fearful visitors that there was no Indian threat in the park. Norris argued vociferously that Native Americans feared geysers and therefore were unwilling to linger in the Yellowstone area.[23] Unfortunately, Norris was so convincing that many historians have presumed that, indeed, Native Americans never used the park's lands. Nonetheless, Indians often held tribal meetings and religious ceremonies in the area, and Native American hunting parties frequented the Yellowstone region.[24] Mark Spence, a historian who has studied Native Americans and their connections with national park lands, has noted that the Yellowstone area, which was viewed as worthless by whites, was quite useful to Native Americans. Norris, however, did everything in his power to convince the federal government to limit Indian access to the park, and in 1880 he negotiated treaties in which two Indian groups agreed to avoid the Yellowstone area.[25]

In any case, Sheridan's interest in Yellowstone was more than fleeting. After hearing the glowing reports from the Washburn Expedition, Sheridan authorized military reconnaissance missions in the area in 1872, 1873, and 1875. In his effort to publicize the threats that hunting and commercialization posed to the park, Sheridan orchestrated a presidential visit to Yellowstone in 1883. Sheridan and President Arthur were accompanied by Secretary of War Robert Lincoln, Senator George G. Vest, Montana's governor, and a seventy-five-man cavalry escort. Sheridan even enlisted Vest's help in a futile attempt to convince Congress to expand the park to protect more game.[26] Sheridan's enthusiasm for Yellowstone would pave the way for military control of the park.

Military intervention in the park was not without precedent. In 1875, Secretary of War William Belknap toured the park with Lieutenant Doane of the Washburn Expedition as a guide. In 1877, the army chased the Nez Perce through the park. That same year, William Tecumseh Sherman and his staff toured the area. In 1880, the Army Corps of Engineers began road construction projects within the park. Superintendent Norris even requested military protection for Yellowstone's natural wonders. Nonetheless, Congress did not seriously consider providing troops until 1883.

Philip Sheridan believed that the army could provide park management that was not subject to the political pressure that the civilian administrations experienced. Unlike civilians, army officers who served as park administrators would not have to depend on the whim of Congress to keep their jobs. It was also not unreasonable to expect the army to fulfill such a nonmilitary mission. After all, the army had already conducted scientific expeditions into frontier areas.

Not surprisingly, political intrigue and conflict ultimately undermined the civilian superintendents of Yellowstone. In 1882, Superintendent Patrick Conger raised the ire of Secretary of the Interior H. M. Teller when he opposed the secretary's decision to grant a park concession monopoly to the Yellowstone National Park Improvement Company. By voicing his objections, Conger made powerful enemies. Eventually, Conger was forced from his position by charges of corruption and incompetence that were leveled against him by the company's management.[27]

D. W. Wear, Yellowstone's last civilian superintendent in the nineteenth century, showed great promise as an administrator. Unfortunately, Wear would also become a victim of politics. Wear's troubles began when a group of junketing congressmen submitted a report that criticized Wear for his inability to protect the park from vandals. While Wear was commended for his exemplary performance in protecting the forests "from fire and axe,"[28] he still struggled to police the park effectively without adequate laws, staff, or funding.

Ironically, Wear's attempts to bring law and order to the park drew fire from Congress. In 1884, Wyoming extended its laws to Yellowstone Park, and Wear began to turn vandals over to the state for prosecution. In 1885, Special Agent for the Department of the Interior W. H. Phillips reported to Congress that such prosecutions were a farce because justices of the peace in Wyoming could retain the fines that they collected in these cases. Phillips was "particularly incensed" that some Yellowstone visitors "of the highest respectability" had been arrested and fined for acts of vandalism.[29] With this report as ammunition, congressmen who were already opposed to making appropriations to the park gained the political support needed to kill further funding for Yellowstone.

Fortunately, the park was not left without protection when Congress withheld funding. After Sheridan's and President Arthur's highly publicized tour of Yellowstone, Congress had added a clause to the 1883 park appropriation bill that would allow the secretary of the interior to call upon the secretary of war for troops to police the park. By withholding funds, Congress forced the secretary of the interior to call for the War Department's help.[30] Thus, the cavalry, under the direction of the Interior Department, assumed control of the park in 1886.

The park's most adamant supporters hoped that the military would serve as temporary protection for the park until a competent and well-funded civilian force could be established at Yellowstone. This "temporary" arrangement would last more than thirty years. Although the military men who served in Yellowstone had no more experience or training in environmental management than had the civilian administrators before them, they demonstrated a sincere commitment to the park's protection. Like Sheridan, they believed that it was the army's duty to protect Yellowstone as a symbol of America's frontier heritage.

The problems that had plagued the civilian managers of Yellowstone were still present when Captain Moses Harris and his men assumed control of the park in August 1886. Indeed, during his first two months as superintendent, Harris reported that hunters had set fires to flush out game and that every notable formation in the park had a "mutilation or defacement." Harris noted that even a simple pencil mark on a geyser would be preserved for years under silica deposits.[31] One of Harris's first acts as superintendent was to formulate a set of rules and regulations for the park. These regulations prohibited the defacement of formations, the cutting of timber, and hunting. Harris even targeted Bannock Indian hunting parties that strayed into the park, arguing that they both threatened the park's fauna and postponed the day that the Indians would become "civilized."[32] The army thus continued its efforts to remove the Indian "threat" to the park. In the park's earliest days, the Indians were perceived as a danger to tourists. By the turn of the century, their hunting practices were viewed as a threat to this managed wilderness.

Even though the army still did not have the legal machinery needed to enforce park rules and regulations, the cavalry was more organized and disciplined, and therefore more effective at policing the parks, than the civilian force had been. Soldiers were far more capable than civilians in compelling rule violators to leave the park or to make restitution for the damage they had caused. Often the superintendent would find creative ways to punish violators through extralegal means. Captain George Anderson kept a poacher in custody for over a month, "awaiting the Secretary's orders."

Anderson eventually released the man—after he confiscated all of the hunter's property. Anderson concluded that this episode would help to "encourage" the majority of hunters to ply their trade outside of the park's boundaries.[33] As Harris's and Anderson's efforts to curb big game hunting demonstrate, the park's mission by the late 1880s had expanded beyond the preservation of wonders and freaks of nature to include the protection of wildlife.

Surprisingly, much of the impetus for making the park a game reserve came from sportsmen—particularly wealthy hunters from the East. One of the most notable defenders of Yellowstone's buffalo was George Bird Grinnell, the editor of *Forest and Stream*. Grinnell, who valued the buffalo both as a symbol of the American frontier and as a prized trophy for the genteel American sportsman, worried that the animals' numbers were dwindling. He believed therefore that the park should be at least one place where buffalo could thrive unmolested.[34]

While the untamed characteristics of the park may have been a nuisance for tourists who expected a certain level of comfort when they traveled, Grinnell saw the park's lack of development as an aid to wildlife protection. Grinnell also argued that the natural increase of buffalo within the park would be beneficial for sportsmen who wanted to hunt them, because some of the animals would eventually stray beyond the park's boundaries.[35] His campaign was thus spurred by both sentimentality and self-interest.

Many of the early park administrators' difficulties in developing a wildlife management policy stemmed from the vague wording of the legislation that had created Yellowstone National Park. According to the park act, Yellowstone simply was supposed to protect game from "wanton" destruction. Of course, the exact definition of wanton was subject to a host of interpretations. In 1882, George Grinnell editorialized against the Yellowstone Valley Hunting Club, a concessionaire that virtually guaranteed its tourist/hunter clients a trophy buffalo. By 1883, however, Secretary of the Interior William Teller had forbidden the killing or capture of wild animals within the park's borders.[36] Eventually the difficult task of enforcing this mandate fell to the cavalry.

Thus, the army officers who served as park superintendents were charged with protecting a de facto wildlife reserve as well as a natural monument and a recreation area. Soldiers protected both game and geysers. The army's policy of confiscating a hunter's equipment helped to curb the poaching of elk, bear, and buffalo in the park. The superintendents also established patrol stations in the park and had them manned during the park's most active tourist months. Eventually, winter outposts also were established, and soldiers patrolled the park on skis.[37]

While Grinnell and sportsmen like him hoped that the army's new role as wildlife protector would expand the population of the nation's buffalo and other "noble" game, park superintendent Captain F. A. Boutelle indulged the interests of sportsmen even further. He encouraged U.S. Fish Commissioner Marshall McDonald to stock Yellowstone's rivers and streams with trout. In 1890, Boutelle, who had been concerned about the "barrenness" of the park's waterways, was pleased to report to the Interior Department that seven thousand trout had been released into park rivers and that one hundred thousand more young trout and salmon would be released soon.[38] Boutelle's successor later marveled at the success of this undertaking. Obviously, this project benefited the visitors who enjoyed fishing for sport. It also demonstrated that those animals that enhanced visitors' experiences were the ones that received the most attention from Yellowstone's managers.

In spite of their limited expertise in wildlife management, the army officers who served as park superintendents were committed to the park. The soldiers assigned to the park seemed quite willing to perform the novel and often unpleasant tasks associated with park upkeep. Unlike other cavalrymen, these soldiers were policemen, tour guides, and firefighters. Captain Boutelle commended his men for the discipline and organization they displayed in fighting fires. Boutelle noted in his annual report that his men "could ride all night and fight fire all the next day" and do so "cheerfully."[39] Captain Harris noted with pride that his men willingly collected garbage and removed "unsightly" objects from geysers, springs, and other points-of-interest. The superintendent believed that this was "a labor of love on the part of the soldiers," for these activities could not "be considered any part of their duty" to the park.[40]

Obviously, the officers tended to accentuate the positive in their reports to Congress. Nonetheless, the army, by virtue of its superior organization and its ability to function without direct appropriations to the park, proved to be a better policing force for Yellowstone than its previous civilian guardians had been. The military had some success in protecting the park's "wonders" from vandals and in protecting buffalo and other wildlife.

The army's emphasis on patrolling the park to prevent poaching and vandalism was perpetuated by civilian superintendents and park rangers long after the cavalry left Yellowstone in 1916. Captain Harris and his successors indeed did have some notion that the interests of tourists should be balanced with a concern for environmental protection. Harris believed that "this 'wonderland' should for all time be kept as nearly as possible in its natural and primitive condition," for "no art and no expenditure of money" could improve upon it.[41]

Nonetheless, Yellowstone was created, first and foremost, to protect natural monuments, not "primitive" nature, however one might define it. Many of the army's efforts to defend and improve the park, such as protecting buffalo from hunters, stocking rivers with fish, and building roads within the park, ultimately focused on the comfort of sightseers and the concerns of sportsmen, rather than environmental protection. This would prove to be a recurring theme in the national parks, as the recreational interests of tourists would take precedence in the nation's second national park, on Mackinac Island, as well.

While modern-day Americans may celebrate Yellowstone as America's first success story in wilderness conservation, this seemingly pristine sample of nature was managed by the U.S. Army in order to protect desirable animals and "monuments" and to increase public access to the park's attractions. Ironically, the army also removed "primitive" native peoples, who had long been associated with wilderness lands by whites, in order to preserve a "wilderness" for today's Americans.

THREE

The "Gem of the Straits" Becomes a National Park

Mackinac Island

In 1875, Congress established the country's second national park on Mackinac Island. Mackinac National Park stood apart from other nineteenth-century parks because of its small size, its Great Lakes location, its status as a military reservation, and its large number of summer visitors. Because of these characteristics, and because the island retained its national park status for only twenty years, historians of the park system have tended to overlook Mackinac Island, or have relegated its national park to footnotes.[1] Nonetheless, the park's origins and management, as well as the island's tourist industry, illustrate the qualities that nineteenth-century Americans revered in nature and deemed worthy of preservation, and reflect the ambiguous status of America's early national parks.

Although different from other early parks, which boasted monumental scenery and offered visitors rugged outdoor adventures, Mackinac had much in common with these western parks. Mackinac, like Yellowstone and Yosemite, was deemed by Congress to be "worthless" for agricultural and industrial (and even military) use. Yet, with its historic fort intact and its reputation for natural beauty, the island indulged the visitor's sense of romance and patriotism. Furthermore, Mackinac's park managers, like other park superintendents, faced the daunting challenge of balancing the interests of tourists with the protection of the island's natural attractions.

Mackinac Island captured the imagination of travelers long before the national park was established. Located in Lake Huron between the upper and lower peninsulas of Michigan, this tiny island had been a hub of trade and travel for centuries. Native Americans called it Michilimackinac, or "Great Turtle," and viewed the island's limestone cliffs as sacred. In the seventeenth century, French explorers, missionaries, and fur trappers passed through the Straits of Mackinac and became the first Europeans to view the island. During the American Revolution, British forces moved their garrison on the mainland near present-day Mackinaw City to a more defensible position on the heights above Mackinac's natural harbor. After the revolution, the United States took control of the island, only to lose it to the British during the War of 1812. The United States regained the island only by treaty after the war.[2]

Mackinac's rich history and natural beauty began to attract summer pleasure travelers in the mid-nineteenth century. While only nine miles in circumference, the island rose three hundred feet above Lake Huron, giving visitors a remarkable view of the Straits of Mackinac. Most vacationers visited the island's celebrated limestone formations, including "Arch Rock," a natural span that rose ninety feet above lake level on the eastern shore of the island. Visitors also traveled by carriage or foot to view the large limestone monolith known as "Sugar Loaf," and examined "Skull Cave," a supposed ancient Indian burial place.[3]

Mackinac's history added to the island's prestige as a tourist Mecca, and the island's military tradition inspired national pride. Visitors eagerly purchased guidebooks to Fort Mackinac from local vendors. Tourists could visit the site where British forces launched the surprise attack on the American garrison in 1812, and enjoy the panoramic view from the site of Fort Holmes on the highest point of the island.

On 11 March 1873, Senator Thomas W. Ferry of Michigan introduced a resolution before the U.S. Senate that would direct the secretary of war to consider designating the Fort Mackinac military reservation as a national park. The park would serve as a "pleasuring ground" for the "benefit and enjoyment" of the American people.[4] Ferry's father had been a missionary on Mackinac, and Thomas Ferry had fond childhood memories of the island and wanted to preserve it for future public enjoyment.[5] (Of course, Congress's endorsement of Mackinac couldn't hurt its reputation as a travel destination.) Ferry defended his proposal by highlighting the island's natural beauty, its historical significance, and its decline in strategic importance.

To achieve his ultimate goal of a national park on Mackinac, Ferry had to convince his fellow senators that the island, like Yellowstone, was both picturesque and devoid of any agricultural or industrial use. Mackinac's waning importance as a military outpost and the decline of the area fur trade since the 1820s both contributed to the perception that the island was valueless, except for its scenery and as a center of tourism.

During his defense of the resolution in the Senate, Ferry acknowledged that the garrison at Mackinac was no longer essential for national security. Indeed, the island's strategic importance had all but disappeared by the mid-nineteenth century. Nonetheless, Ferry argued that the island was historically significant. He noted the French were exploring the Mackinac region at the same time that the Puritans were arriving in New England. He also cited Fort Mackinac's importance during the War of 1812. Ferry maintained that the island was worthy of protection because it embodied America's national heritage.[6]

Ferry emphasized the island's natural charms and geologic curiosities in defense of his proposal, and he maintained that Mackinac's location made it ideal for national park status. He noted that Yellowstone was expansive, but relatively inaccessible. In contrast, Mackinac had been attracting middle- and upper-class visitors from the Midwest and East since midcentury. National park status for Mackinac would simply enhance the island's reputation as a resort and put lands that were already under governmental control to the "useful service" of cultivating national pride.[7]

Senator Ferry's resolution did not pass without opposition. While Senator Morgan Hamilton of Texas admitted that he knew little about the island's topography or vegetation, he questioned whether Mackinac had any timber that could be used by private interests in the future. The senator was not wholly convinced that the United States should create national parks for the preservation of scenery when the land could be used for some practical purpose. He stated that a national park was nothing "but a sink-hole to waste money in," and warned his fellow senators that the United States could not afford to preserve every historic site.[8]

Ferry and his fellow senator from Michigan assured their colleagues that Mackinac was worthless for anything other than public enjoyment. Ferry stated unequivocally that "there is no timber upon that island that is

worth anything as timber." Senator Zachariah Chandler of Michigan supported Ferry's assertion, arguing that Mackinac was "simply a watering
place." Claiming that the island was only "a rock out in the lake a few miles,
with . . . very little vegetation," Chandler still pronounced it "a romantic
spot, visited by people from all parts of the United States." Following the
debate, the resolution passed by a vote of thirty-seven to thirteen.[9]

Major O. M. Poe of the Corps of Engineers was assigned the task of eval-
uating the island's suitability for national park status. In his report to Secretary of War William Belknap, Poe stated that the island was no longer
strategically important. He also acknowledged that the "salubrity of its summer climate and the beauty of its scenery" made Mackinac an ideal summer
resort. Poe believed that as long as the island was available for military purposes, there could be no objection to the dedication of a park on Mackinac.[10]

Senator Ferry's proposal was eventually endorsed by Belknap. With the
War Department's blessing, Ferry strongly campaigned for the passage of the
Mackinac National Park bill. On 28 May 1874, the Senate passed this bill
and sent it to the House of Representatives.

During the final debate on 3 March 1875, the bill faced opposition similar to that it had faced in the Senate. While Representative William Conger
of Michigan vigorously defended the bill, Representative William Holman
of Indiana still feared the expense that a national park on Mackinac might
entail. When Martin Maginnis, the delegate from Montana, reminded him
that Yellowstone had not cost the government a dollar, Holman stated that
he opposed the concept of federal responsibility for maintaining recreation
areas.[11] In the end, two-thirds of the representatives voted in favor of preserving Mackinac's "curiosities," and President Grant signed the measure
into law.

Mackinac's scenic value and industrial worthlessness thus made it an
attractive candidate for national park status. Furthermore, the creation of
the park entailed no additional outlay of funds, because the reserve could
be superimposed on a military site. The founding of a national park even
encouraged the island's booming tourist trade, which had been Mackinac's
major industry since midcentury.[12] Indeed, tourism made productive use of
seemingly "worthless" limestone formations and an antiquated military
reservation on a tiny island in Lake Huron.

Ironically, Mackinac's future as a protected area hinged upon its continued "worthlessness." As in the case of Yellowstone National Park, Congress reserved the right to rescind the Mackinac National Park Act if the land
was found to possess more than aesthetic value. Indeed, section three of the

measure stated that the park "shall be at all times available for military purposes" and acknowledged the possibility that the act could be repealed in
the future.[13] Of course, it was logical for the Department of War, as administrator of the park, to have complete access to these public lands for the
staging of military operations. National park status therefore would not
eliminate the possibility of future military use of the island, nor would the
park act guarantee Mackinac's integrity if the island were found to possess
some agricultural or industrial value.

Like their congressional representatives, most U.S. citizens were indif-
ferent to the concept of natural preservation. Nonetheless, Americans'
appreciation of nature grew as the nation's "frontier" areas disappeared. By
the second half of the nineteenth century, many intellectuals feared that
urban-based Americans did not possess the strength, virtue, or stamina of
their ancestors. While urban Americans viewed the progress of "civilization" favorably, they were sufficiently removed from the wilderness to look
upon their country's "frontier" past with nostalgia.[14]

Americans therefore began to view contact with nature as a means of
recapturing the moral and spiritual qualities of the nation's earliest settlers.[15]
Transcendentalists, in particular, believed that America should preserve a
sample of nature in order to reconcile the conflict between wilderness and
civilization.[16] Most nineteenth-century nature lovers, however, did not wish
to escape the trappings of civilization completely. For example, Henry David
Thoreau believed that the man who always lived in the wilderness was too
primitive to fully appreciate nature.[17] Mackinac's "civilized" visitors therefore wished to contemplate scenery in comfort and enjoy the health benefits
that nature had to offer, not reacquaint themselves with untamed wilderness.
Mackinac was the best of both the civilized and natural worlds—a luxury
resort that offered a glimpse of American pioneer history.

Senator Ferry proposed the establishment of the national park with the
hope that Mackinac's historical significance would not be lost to future generations. The summer visitors who had been flocking to the island for
decades also appreciated the aesthetic qualities of the island's limestone formations, for they supposedly represented the natural beauty of wild America. These tourists believed that contact with nature would engender a new
appreciation for beauty, strengthen moral and spiritual values, and reaffirm
nationalistic pride in America's frontier past.

Romantic images of nature abounded in nineteenth-century descriptions of Mackinac. Tributes such as "Gem of the Straits," "Fairy Isle," "Beau-
teous Isle," "Tourists' Paradise," and "Princess of the Islands" were applied

liberally by enthusiastic visitors, pamphleteers, and amateur historians.[18] Indeed, Mackinac did enchant many of its visitors, for the island was a symbol of wild nature in the increasingly industrialized, urbanized Midwest.

In the second half of the nineteenth century, writers were wholeheartedly endorsing Mackinac as a vacation paradise. Here, they claimed, pallid-cheeked city dwellers could restore both body and soul by enjoying outdoor activities that brought them into contact with nature. Middle- and upper-class visitors were encouraged to help Mackinac fishermen with their nets, or to take an "airing" along island paths in a cart "drawn by a French pony, with a ragged half-breed for a driver." Such activities would surely provide mental and physical release from the "anxieties of an active business life."[19]

Another attraction for Mackinac's summer visitors was the island's reputation as a health resort. By the mid-nineteenth century, Americans who were seeking physical rejuvenation flocked to vacation spots where the air was clean and the water pure.[20] Much of Mackinac's popularity with health-seeking tourists stemmed from its mild summer climate and its natural beauty.

Few nineteenth-century commentators failed to mention the island's supposed restorative qualities. Reverend James Van Fleet reported that the island's "cool air and pure water, together with its natural beauties and historic associations, are just what are needed to bring back the glow of health to the faded cheek."[21] Fort Mackinac's former post surgeon claimed that the island's mild summer climate cured diseases "peculiar to hot weather . . . as if by magic." Even patients in the late stages of consumption or wasting thoracic diseases were often "greatly benefited," in his estimation.[22] Many believed that simply taking pleasure in Mackinac's natural beauty would have positive effects on health. Physicians would not have to prescribe "health-making gymnastics" on Mackinac, but merely direct their patients "to walk about and enjoy the sights and scenes about them, to saunter along its winding paths, or go fishing."[23]

The experiences of William Cullen Bryant during a visit to Mackinac in 1846 embodied much of the romanticism and health benefit that most mid-century tourists hoped to experience on the island. During his stay, Bryant and a party of other tourists visited the principal historic sites and "curiosities" on the island. Bryant noted Mackinac's historical significance as a center for the fur trade, delighted in the island's "picturesque" woodland paths, and enjoyed the "proverbial" health benefits of northern Michigan's "pure and elastic" air. He firmly believed that "the world has not many islands so beautiful as Mackinaw."[24] For Bryant, such natural beauty was a source of national identity and pride.[25] Like Senator Ferry, Bryant viewed Mackinac as a symbol of America's heritage.

While Bryant and Mackinac's other summer visitors came to the island to experience the purifying effects of nature, they did not want to escape the trappings of civilization altogether. For the nineteenth-century tourist, Mackinac, like Yellowstone, offered natural curiosities for sightseeing. Visitors did not travel to Mackinac simply to enjoy the wild outdoors, but to experience the striking scenic characteristics (and health benefits) that the island had to offer. Ironically, but inevitably, Mackinac's reputation for unspoiled natural beauty led to a greater commercialization of the island.

The number of visitors to Mackinac increased as rail and steamship transportation developed. The majority of the national park's visitors traveled by steamship from major Great Lakes ports such as Cleveland, Detroit, Duluth, and Chicago, or traveled by rail to the Straits of Mackinac and then proceeded to the island by ferry. Between 1875 and 1895, approximately 70 percent of the island's hotel guests came from Michigan, Illinois, and Ohio. Over 90 percent of the cottage owners were from Michigan and Illinois.[26] Mackinac was therefore a summer resort for a primarily Midwestern clientele. Of course, national park status only enhanced Mackinac's reputation.

The length of a Mackinac visitor's stay could range from a few hours to the entire summer. As Mackinac's tourist traffic increased during the late nineteenth century, the island's hotels and boardinghouses stood ready to accommodate the traveler for a few nights or the whole season. The most luxurious of these was the Grand Hotel. Built by railroad and steamship interests and opened in 1887, the Grand cemented Mackinac's status as a fashionable resort.[27]

No matter how brief their visit, tourists desired to see Mackinac's "curiosities." Carriage tours of the island were therefore exceptionally popular, and liveries conducted a booming business. Numerous restaurants and shops catered to the tourists' wants. Maple sugar candy, moccasins, baskets, "Indian" novelties, and stereographic pictures of landmarks were some of the most popular souvenirs among tourists.[28]

Quite obviously, Mackinac National Park did not offer its visitors a rugged, wilderness experience. However, the expectations of Mackinac visitors in many ways were similar to those of Yellowstone's small cadre of tourists. Both groups wanted to visit particular natural points-of-interest and be edified by the experience; both viewed the parks as the embodiment of the nation's frontier heritage; both wanted to escape urban environments; and both hoped to experience the mental and physical benefits that the parks supposedly offered. Furthermore, as in the case of Yellowstone National Park, the Department of War would provide for the wants of Mackinac's visitors.

According to the congressional act that established Mackinac National Park, the park lands were "under the exclusive control" of the Department of War. The commandant of Fort Mackinac, who was also the park superintendent, was charged with establishing rules and regulations for the park, protecting the island's natural attractions and wildlife, and expanding and developing the island's roads and bridle paths.[29] The superintendent was also responsible for raising much of the revenue needed to execute these missions.

Major Alfred L. Hough, Mackinac post commandant, in consultation with the Corps of Engineers, composed the rules and regulations for the park. These rules prohibited individuals from injuring or defacing trees, "natural curiosities," or governmental postings or structures within the park. Hunting, shooting, and disorderly or obscene conduct were also prohibited. An individual guilty of any of these offenses would be ejected from the park.

The new park manager was fortunate because he did not have a large tract of land to protect. There also was no big game on the island to make poaching a significant problem. (Western park managers would not be so lucky.) This did not, however, mean that his job was an easy one. Mackinac's superintendent would have to cater to the needs of thousands of summer visitors while simultaneously protecting the park from both tourists and local citizens.

One of the many other challenges that the commandant faced as a national park supervisor was a chronic shortage of funds. As in the case of Yellowstone National Park, Congress provided no money for park development or maintenance. Mackinac, however, already had a built-in ranger force of soldiers from the fort, and the Department of War provided funds for the upkeep of the military reservation. Even though Mackinac's superintendent often complained that he lacked sufficient monetary support for park projects, he was far better off than N. P. Langford, who had no staff or direct funding for Yellowstone.

Along with his duties of protecting the island's attractions and providing for the comfort and safety of park visitors, the commandant had to raise much of the revenue needed to execute these missions. As a means of raising capital, Congress gave the park superintendent the authority to grant leases of small parcels of land for the building of summer cottages. By 1892, twenty-seven lots had been surveyed and leased to summer visitors, on the condition that the lessee would improve the land within a year. Most of these lots were on the bluffs, and had a spectacular view of Lake Huron. The rental for these plots was twenty-five dollars per year. The remaining rear lots, which were less desirable because they possessed a view of the cottages' refuse heaps and outhouses, were leased at fifteen dollars per year for the construction of stables.[30] The proceeds from these leases were a major source of revenue for the park. In the twentieth century, these picturesque Victorian cottages became as much of an attraction as the fort and the island's limestone formations.

Nevertheless, the money generated by rentals was inadequate to finance road repairs and general park maintenance. Although the superintendent often lobbied for additional funds, the War Department took a dim view of expenditures for the national park. Indeed, the War Department was unwilling to allocate funds beyond the "legitimate military expenses" associated with fort maintenance. The department's ambivalent attitude toward the park stemmed from the knowledge that Congress had increased the army's responsibilities at Mackinac without raising its appropriations accordingly. The War Department also believed that the two companies stationed at Fort Mackinac could be utilized more effectively on the western frontier.[31]

The park superintendent did have another major source of revenue, however. In 1884, the secretary of the interior and Congress approved the sale of Fort Mackinac's wood reservation on nearby Bois Blanc Island, with the proceeds to be set aside for the benefit of the national park.[32] In December 1891, park superintendent E. M. Coates urged the secretary of war to expedite these sales, for valuable timber on the unsold lots was being stripped away by private parties.[33] Clearly, Bois Blanc Island's value rested in its timber and not in its beauty as a wilderness area. Thus, a "valuable" piece of property was utilized to preserve a "worthless" watering place. While Bois Blanc actually embodied the characteristics of wilderness and the Michigan frontier, its forests were sacrificed to protect a tourist Mecca and resort that served as a museum to that frontier past. Visitors simply wanted a glimpse of this past—from the comfort of a passenger ferry or the front porch of a luxury hotel. They did not want the unadulterated wilderness experience.

Park funding was not the superintendent's only worry. Much of the superintendent's time and energy were devoted to protecting Mackinac from wanton vandalism. He was constantly harried by both tourists and island residents who damaged the island's trees and rock formations. Fort commandant E. M. Coates reported depredations, such as the peeling of white birch trees and the destruction of park benches and signs, to the secretary of war.[34] Unfortunately, efforts to curb such acts were hampered by the War Department's unwillingness to allocate extra duty pay to the fort's garrison for patrolling the park. It was also nearly impossible to catch a visitor in the act of obtaining a "souvenir" from a limestone formation or a tree.[35]

Tourists were not entirely to blame for damage done to the park. Mackinac's small contingent of full-time residents also wreaked havoc on the island's landscape. Islanders cut down trees and grazed cattle illegally on park lands. The cattle proved exceptionally annoying to the superintendent. These animals blocked roads, trampled vegetation, and fouled the island's supposedly pure, medicinal air. The commandant expressed his concerns to both his superiors and local officials, to little avail.[36]

Ironically, islanders damaged Mackinac's natural beauty even though they depended upon tourism for their livelihoods. Unfortunately, some dubious park "improvements" also threatened the character of the "curiosities" that made the island worthy of national park status. Shortly before the arrival of Fort Mackinac's new commandant in 1884, Lieutenant Dwight Kelton undertook the removal of roots protruding from Sugar Loaf and the clearing of bushes around Arch Rock. After a visitor charged that this work "vandalized" these island landmarks, Kelton explained to his superiors that tourists could now view Arch Rock without alighting from their carriages and could enjoy the "majesty" of Sugar Loaf without obstructions. Clearly, Kelton believed that his duties to the park included the "improvement" of natural attractions. Nonetheless, Captain George K. Brady and Secretary of War Lincoln took a dim view of Kelton's activities. After this incident, Lincoln required that all park construction be approved by the Department of War.[37]

Kelton's actions serve as an extreme example of a park manager's willingness to alter the natural landscape in an attempt to cater to the presumed wants of tourists. Nevertheless, any park development that provided for tourists' safety or convenience had an impact on the island's terrain, and the superintendent had to weigh the relative merits of each project accordingly. This could be a potentially frustrating task for the commandant, for he had no precedent in national park management to look to for guidance.

In spite of this handicap, Mackinac National Park's superintendents generally did a respectable job of providing for public safety and enjoyment. Even though park funds were "entirely inadequate," commandants such as E. M. Coates were able to widen and grade roads, construct park benches, maintain park signs, and provide safety rails on the island's east bluffs.[38]

Years before the National Park Service was established, however, the army abandoned its position as park caretaker on Mackinac Island. For twenty years, the Department of War had protected and maintained an out-post that possessed little strategic military importance for the sake of the national park. In the 1890s, however, Mackinac became the victim of a general reduction in manned army outposts. As western frontier lands were settled and Reconstruction came to an end, the army placed greater emphasis on manning coastal fortifications and protecting the United States from foreign threats. By 1891, the army had abandoned one-quarter of the posts it had occupied in 1889.[39] Secretary of War Daniel Lamont concluded in 1894 that his department could no longer justify the forty- to fifty-thousand-dollar annual allocation needed to maintain Fort Mackinac and protect the national park. As the War Department and Congress debated over Fort Mackinac's fate, the army removed most of the fort's garrison and field guns to Fort Brady at Sault Ste. Marie, leaving only a squad of eleven men and their commander to guard the fort and national park.[40]

By 1895, Congress realized that twelve men could not offer effective protection for the national park. The commanding general of the army, Lieutenant General John M. Schofield, indicated that the army could not afford to manage the park in the future. In a letter written to Michigan Senator McMillan, Schofield stated that the army's involvement in nonmilitary activities such as park management could leave it unprepared for a military emergency.[41] Congress now faced the task of establishing and funding a civilian ranger force on the island if it hoped to preserve the national park.

Instead of providing the money and manpower needed to protect and manage Mackinac, Congress decided to abdicate all responsibility for the reserve. Fearing that the federal government would sell the park to private interests, the House of Representatives and the Senate of the State of Michigan lobbied vigorously against the repeal of Mackinac's national park status.[42] In lieu of selling the military reserve, Congress decided to give Fort Mackinac and the island's government lands to the State of Michigan, with the stipulation that the former national park be maintained as a state park. The Michigan legislature accepted the national government's gift, and Mackinac Island State Park was born.[43]

On 31 May 1895, the Michigan legislature created the Mackinac Island State Park Commission to govern the new state reserve. Thomas W. Ferry was appointed to the body and served as its first president. Ironically, the state did not appropriate funds for the park. The commissioners lobbied the Department of War for funds, but War Secretary Lamont rejected their appeals, for park protection and maintenance were now nonmilitary activities. The commission eventually solved its cash flow problems by raising the rent on park properties.[44]

The efforts and achievements of the national park's military superintendents helped the new state park on Mackinac Island. Even though the army had abandoned Fort Mackinac, island visitors were still fascinated by the old outpost. The army's previous maintenance and preservation efforts helped ensure that the fort would be a tourist attraction in future years. In 1915, the park commission turned the fort into a museum. Visitors could now enjoy exhibits of Native American and pioneer artifacts as they explored the fort's blockhouses, officers' quarters, and parade grounds. In the 1930s, the commission utilized the Civilian Conservation Corps in an effort to maintain the fort. Eventually, the commission established an interpretive museum in the fort that depicted army life on the island.[45]

The new state park inherited many improvements from the island's former caretakers. The army left a well-developed system of trails, bridle paths, and roads as a legacy to the State of Michigan. Safety rails, park benches, and other amenities were also in place when the army surrendered the park to the state. The commission continued the army's tradition of park development. It reconstructed the blockhouse and garrison on the site of Fort Holmes after the lookout tower erected by the army was destroyed. Park administrators also dedicated tablets and monuments to the island's military heroes, labeled trees and plants of interest to tourists, and banned all automobiles from the island to preserve its air and nineteenth-century charm.

Thus, Mackinac National Park became a footnote in most histories of the U.S. national park system. Indeed, it did not possess the monumental scenery associated with other early parks, such as Yellowstone or Yosemite. Nevertheless, the island's brief life as the nation's second national park is representative of the American romantic ideals of nature. Romantics, health-seekers, and Midwesterners who longed for America's past converged on this tiny island during the summer months in the late nineteenth century. Like other early parks, however, Mackinac's status hinged upon its "worthlessness" for productive enterprise, save tourism.

Mackinac National Park provides examples of the fundamental difficulties faced by early park superintendents. With inadequate funding and few precedents in environmental management to guide their actions, these fort commandants and pioneers in park supervision faced the challenge of "improving" the park for visitors while preserving the appearance of wild, natural beauty in a heavily utilized, highly developed park.

Although Mackinac did not embody the grandeur and monumentalism of Yellowstone, it seemed to provide the spiritual and physical health benefits that late-nineteenth-century travelers expected of natural recreation areas. While historical preservation was not an acknowledged function of the national park system until the 1930s, Mackinac also functioned as a historical monument that inspired national pride in island visitors. Even though the national government abdicated responsibility for protecting the island's natural and historical attractions, the State of Michigan continued to preserve the island "for the health, comfort, and pleasure, for the benefit and enjoyment of the people."[46]

FOUR

Nature's Majestic Marvels

Yosemite, Sequoia, and General Grant

On 28 July 1890, Representative William Vandever of California introduced a bill that would set aside a prominent grove of Sierra Redwoods, also known as giant sequoias, as a "public park or reserve . . . to preserve at least some" of these rare trees. This bill passed with no opposition on 25 September 1890.[1] The following week, on 1 October 1890, Congress passed another bill sponsored by Vandever, which set aside land surrounding California's Yosemite Valley and a small grove of giant sequoias as "reserved forest lands."[2] With these two acts, Sequoia National Park, Yosemite National Park, and General Grant National Park were born.

The legislation that created these three new national parks was similar to the acts that created Yellowstone and Mackinac. The secretary of the interior was directed to establish park rules and regulations and to prevent the wanton destruction of wildlife within the reserves' boundaries. Unfortunately, Congress still did not provide these new parks with the judicial machinery needed to enforce regulations, nor did it provide any funds for park protection or improvements. Although the park legislation did not expressly call for military management of the new parks, Congress assumed that the army would provide protection for them. Secretary of the Interior John Noble also saw the army's intervention in Yellowstone as a precedent for park management, and therefore asked the secretary of war to send two troops of cavalry to the California parks during the summer months.[3] Although the secretary of war initially resisted Noble's appeal because he questioned the legality of the army's involvement in the parks, the cavalry would ultimately protect Yosemite, Sequoia, and General Grant National Parks for more than twenty years.

The creation of these new parks reinforced the monumentalism precedent that had been set by Yellowstone National Park. More importantly, the early history of these three parks demonstrates the limitations of wild land management and protection policies in the nineteenth and early twentieth centuries. Many of the difficulties park managers faced were directly linked to visitors' expectations for (and their activities in) the parks.

While the new national park at Yosemite would encompass as much land as the state of Rhode Island, the national government did not have authority over the celebrated Yosemite Valley or the Mariposa Big Tree Grove of Sequoias. California had controlled the valley and grove as a state park since 1864 and did not surrender its control over the lands until 1906. The state's mismanagement of its park, however, was the impetus for Congress to establish Yosemite National Park around the valley in 1890.

Long before white travelers and the federal government became aware of the Yosemite Valley's existence, various Miwok peoples and Mono-Paiutes, known collectively as the Yosemite Indians, visited the valley in the summer months to gather acorns, medicinal plants, and wild sweet potatoes. Often, native peoples would burn underbrush on the valley floor to encourage the growth of useful plants. These controlled burns also gave the valley open meadows and a somewhat manicured, parklike appearance.[4]

Although the valley was "discovered" by whites during militia campaigns against Native Americans in the early 1850s, the Yosemites managed to maintain a presence in the state and national parks until the 1940s, when tourism and national park regulations forced them out. The valley's name itself bears witness to past conflict between the Native Americans and the white soldiers. For decades, park historians have assumed that the name was related to "Uzumati," the Miwok word for "grizzly bear." The militia invaders of the 1850s apparently believed that the Yosemites were making a flattering comparison between whites and the noble, venerated grizzly bear when they used the word in reference to the soldiers. Today, "Yosemite" is believed to be a corruption of "Yo-che-ma-te," which means "some among them are killers."[5]

White Americans became interested in Yosemite as a travel destination after James Hutchings led the first tourist expedition through the valley in 1855. His published account of the tour assured Yosemite's fame in the West. In 1859, Yosemite caught the attention of easterners after Horace Greeley pronounced the valley, with spectacular waterfalls at one end and Half Dome at the other, "the most unique and majestic of nature's marvels."[6]

Fearing that the valley would be claimed by homesteaders, who would destroy its beauty or exploit it for tourist dollars, Senator John Conness of California introduced a bill that would grant the Yosemite Valley and the Mariposa Big Tree Grove to the State of California. The state would hold the lands "for public use, resort, and recreation." The park would be managed by nine commissioners, including the governor of California.[7] The bill was passed easily by Congress and was signed into law by President Lincoln on 30 June 1864. The State of California now controlled eight square miles of the Yosemite Valley and a few hundred acres of Giant Sequoias.

Frederick Law Olmsted, who later achieved fame as the architect of New York's Central Park, chaired the planning commission for the new state park. Olmsted was not necessarily interested in protecting "wilderness" for its own sake. Instead, he believed that nature could provide health benefits and an escape from the stresses of urban life. Olmsted felt that the contemplation of Yosemite's magnificent scenery would uplift the spirit and strengthen the moral fiber of urban Americans.[8]

Olmsted wanted to increase public access to the park while keeping intrusive construction projects, which would distract the visitors' attention from the natural scenery, to a minimum. Olmsted's ideal was to blend park amenities with the environment, and to conceal development as much as possible. In his formal proposal for park management and development, Olmsted pushed for the construction of a one-way circuit trail around the valley, which would be hidden from view. He argued for free public access to the park, and believed that a few rustic cabins could be built for visitors with minimum disturbance to Yosemite's natural beauty. Olmsted also wanted the commission to monitor closely all concessions in the park.[9]

The park's governing board and the State of California never acted on Olmsted's proposals. Olmsted left to work on Central Park soon after he submitted his report, and some of the other park commissioners suppressed his proposals, in part because they had financial interests in park concessions.

The Yosemite State Park Commission's ability to manage the park effectively was also hampered by the lack of state funding. Without funds, the commission could not undertake any major road-building projects or trail improvements. Consequently, Yosemite's visitors would travel over rude, undeveloped paths until the national park was established. The state had stipulated that the commissioners could hire a "guardian" for the park, yet the legislature did not pay the guardian's meager wages on time.[10]

The commissioners did have the option of granting leases within the park to generate funds. Unfortunately, their leasing practices soon drew fire from the state legislature. Charges of graft and favoritism in the granting of leases drove the governor to dissolve the board and appoint a new one in 1880. The board clearly did not hold the preservation of the park's natural beauty as a high ideal when leasing park lands. The commission leased sections of the valley to individuals who turned forests and meadows into hayfields, garden plots, pigsties, and hotel refuse heaps.[11]

Yosemite did, however, have an ardent defender in John Muir. Muir, who founded the Sierra Club in 1892, discovered the Sierra Nevada Mountains and the Yosemite Valley for himself in the late 1860s. Although Muir is one of the best known and most admired environmental activists of the nineteenth century, his love of "wilderness" contrasted markedly with most other Americans' opinions of nature. Muir believed in protecting nature for its sublime characteristics at a time when the majority of Americans viewed the natural world in terms of its utility.

Muir believed that Yosemite Park suffered from gross mismanagement. Without a staff or funding, the park's guardian was virtually powerless to stop what Muir perceived to be the greatest threat to the Yosemite area—sheep. Although he had once worked as a herder in the Sierras, a repentant Muir claimed that these "hoofed locusts" consumed all vegetation in their path and destroyed the habitat of wild animals in the park.[12] He also denounced the sheepherders' practice of burning over acres of Yosemite lands to encourage the growth of grass for the next year's grazing.

Muir's anger prompted him to take action on behalf of the park. Muir enlisted the help of Robert Underwood Johnson, the associate editor of *The Century* magazine. Muir's articles, which denounced the destruction of forestlands in and around the Yosemite Valley, became prominent features in Johnson's magazine.[13]

The publicity that Muir generated for the area encouraged Congress to establish Yosemite National Park around the valley and the Mariposa Grove. The Yosemite State Park would remain a separate reserve within the national park. Congress left the valley in the hands of the state, assuming that California would resist as a matter of state pride federal attempts to reclaim the reserve. Indeed, sixteen years would pass before the state would relinquish its claim on the park.

On 6 April 1891, Captain Abram E. "Jug" Wood, commander of Troop I of the Fourth Cavalry, became superintendent of the newly formed Yosemite National Park. Wood later reported to the secretary of the interior that he "had no idea" what his duties to the park would be, for such responsibilities "were entirely new" to him.[14]

Wood immediately contacted the stock owners in the area and asked them to stay clear of Yosemite. In spite of his efforts to discourage grazing in the park, however, sheepherders continued to challenge Wood's authority. Wood curbed much of the illegal grazing by making an example of a few herders. When Wood's troops arrested four men for illegally grazing sheep in the park, the superintendent proceeded to telegraph for a deputy U.S. marshal. Wood had no intention of turning the prisoners over to the marshal, but he sent the wire "for effect." Eventually, Wood allowed the men to post bond.[15] These maneuvers, along with the vigilance of the troops patrolling the park, greatly reduced the incidence of such trespass in Yosemite.

Wood's successors would find equally ingenious methods of punishing herders. Soldiers would often expel a herder and his sheep from the park, but not at the same boundary. Thus, mountains and miles of travel could separate the trespasser from his livestock. Such extralegal methods to enforce the rules convinced at least a few sheepherders and owners that it would be cheaper to locate another grazing range.[16]

Although Yosemite did not have a great deal of large game in comparison with Yellowstone, the park's administrators were still concerned with protecting game animals from poachers. In 1896, Colonel S. B. M. Young ordered his men to confiscate firearms from tourists in an effort to eliminate hunting in Yosemite. Young hoped that the park would become a refuge for wildlife and a place where animals could be studied in their natural state.[17] Yosemite's military superintendents were also active in efforts to stock the park's rivers and lakes with fish.

Major John Bigelow Jr. became a true innovator in park development when he constructed a one-hundred-acre arboretum and botanical garden in Yosemite. By the fall of 1904, Bigelow's men had transplanted a variety of plants to the arboretum, labeled many trees, and constructed paths and benches for the gardens. The superintendent believed that "one of the essential purposes of the Yosemite forest reservation was to provide a museum of nature for the general public free of cost."[18]

Bigelow's arboretum was excluded from Yosemite when the park's borders were redrawn in 1905 to make way for a railroad line. The park boundaries had been redrawn a few years before to accommodate mining interests as well. For Congress, the national park's primary function was to provide a buffer zone around the picturesque Yosemite Valley; excess forestlands therefore could be eliminated from the park if the need arose.[19] The preservation of monumental beauty, rather than the protection of wild lands or representative ecosystems, was the primary goal.

It is quite apparent that the army men who served in Yosemite were dedicated to the park. It is also easy, however, to overestimate the army's success in land management when its record is compared to that of the state park commission. The state park commissioners, who controlled the valley until 1906, had to deal with the bulk of the tourist traffic, and the problems brought by campers and concessionaires.[20] The cavalry's major responsibility was policing the lands surrounding the valley, which it did do effectively. Soldiers did not have to cater to so many of the wants of visitors, and therefore were not subject to the same criticisms leveled at the state park officials. The army did, however, create a rugged image for park caretakers that would be attached to park rangers long after the National Park Service was created. Many of the early rangers employed by the park service were former soldiers, and patrolling reserves and protecting them from fire have been viewed as distinctly masculine activities.[21]

On 14 May 1891, Troop K of the Fourth Cavalry left San Francisco for Sequoia National Park. These soldiers were charged with protecting both Sequoia and nearby General Grant National Park. As in Yosemite National Park, the army remained in these parks only during the tourist season. Inclement weather was left to protect the parks in the winter.

Unlike at Yellowstone or Mackinac, the curiosities of Sequoia and General Grant were not geological. The parks' massive trees were "peculiar" enough to become a tourist attraction, however, and Congress's efforts to establish the parks drew visitors to the area.[22]

General Vandever was prompted to introduce the bills that would create Sequoia National Park and General Grant National Park by a few prominent citizens of Visalia, California, a town fifty miles from the General Grant Grove.[23] These community leaders wanted to save the area sequoias from loggers. Logging operations had been destroying the big trees since the 1860s. Lumbermen cut and dynamited many groves of California Redwoods and Sequoias decades before any effort was made to preserve them. Fortunately, many groves were spared because they were inaccessible to lumbermen. Also, loggers eventually lost interest in the sequoia because its wood was too soft for construction. Through legislative action, a few farsighted Californians ensured that some of the remaining tress would be under the protection of the federal government. The army would serve as guardian for the two parks because of the precedent of military management and protection at Mackinac and Yellowstone.

When Captain Joseph H. Dorst and his men traveled to the newly founded Sequoia National Park in the spring of 1891, they discovered that the main road to the park was virtually impassable in inclement weather. The troop's progress was hindered for days by rain and mud. Upon arriving in the park, Dorst made mapping the park his first priority, because there were no comprehensive maps of the area.[24] While these conditions would, at first, limit visitor access to the park, the area's inaccessibility had saved its giant sequoias from destruction before the park was founded.

Tourists did not pose much of a threat to the integrity of the two "tree parks" in the early years of their existence, because there were few visitors to affect the parks. Also, Americans generally found defacing Yellowstone's limestone curiosities more entertaining than destroying trees. A few of Sequoia and General Grant's visitors, however, were not above peeling the bark off the giant trees or carving their names into them. General Grant Park felt the effects of this vandalism the most because it attracted more tourists than Sequoia—most of them from the San Francisco area. The "General Grant" tree, the park's central attraction, often bore the brunt of visitors' enthusiasm. Before the park was founded, many "admirers" had shot arrows bearing their names into the giant tree. The "General's" bark was also scarred by the burns and carvings of vandals.[25] The superintendent of Sequoia tried to limit such mischief by sending regular patrols to the park. Eventually, fencing would also provide protection for prominent trees.

As in Yosemite, the superintendent found that sheep were the greatest threat to the tree reserves. Soldiers were constantly chasing stray sheep and cattle out of the parks. Captain Dorst firmly believed that the sheep had a negative impact on the reserves even when the animals were kept outside of the parks. Dorst perceived that the sheep drove wild game from the area. He also theorized (erroneously) that the herders' practice of burning over large tracts of brush and timber could lead to flooding and soil erosion.[26] Dorst and his successors called for the enlargement of the parks to protect the habitat of the giant sequoias and the area's wild game. Congress did not respond. The army had to make do with its patrolling efforts.

The army's development of the two parks was rather limited, because Congress made no appropriations until the turn of the century. The army did, however, guard the parks against fire, construct rude trails, and stock area waterways with trout.[27] Regular patrols also limited much of the illegal sheep grazing in the park. The troop's achievements were truly impressive, considering the meager eight-thousand-dollar annual allocation granted by the War Department for all three California parks.[28] The army's positive influence in the area was sorely missed when the troops temporarily abandoned the parks during the Spanish-American War. During the cavalry's absence, Sequoia, General Grant, and Yosemite National Parks were overrun by sheep.[29]

As in Yosemite, the army provided enthusiastic, if not experienced, guardians for Sequoia and General Grant. Dorst, for example, viewed Sequoia Park as "the most remarkable forest of its kind in the world," and believed that "as it stands now . . . it ought to remain."[30] Nonetheless, these army men did not possess any expertise in modern theories of conservation or ecology. What they did have was a vague notion that the parks' ecosystems were best managed by nature itself. Often, however, they did not follow even this unofficial rule.

One of the most problematic issues for park managers was fire control. Colonel S. B. M. Young chose not to "spot burn" foliage during Yosemite's dry season, as the Indians had done in the past, because he thought it might disturb the water table.[31] Unfortunately, the commitment by Young, Dorst, and their troops to fighting forest fires often left an accumulation of underbrush that could encroach on meadows that had existed long before whites had arrived in the area, obstruct views of natural attractions, and most importantly, fuel great conflagrations that would seriously threaten ancient forests.[32] Likewise, the Army's efforts to stock rivers with trout demonstrated a willingness to tamper with the natural environment if it would serve the interests of sportsmen and tourists.

After 1906, when California surrendered control of its state park, the cavalry (and later, the National Park Service) would also have to contend with tourist problems in the Yosemite Valley. One of the greatest threats to the scenic character of the valley was concessions. Yosemite's earliest visitors traveled by horseback into the valley, camped, and brought their own provisions. By the late nineteenth and early twentieth centuries, however, concessionaires argued that the plethora of hotels, general stores, souvenir shops, and photography studios on the valley floor were needed by visitors. The state park commission initially encouraged such development in order to increase tourist traffic. Nonetheless, even questionable park concessions were not restricted after visitation increased, because tourists had come to expect these services. Twentieth-century concessionaires would thus claim that luxury hotels, cocktail lounges, swimming pools, beauty salons, stage performances, and "fireworks" displays (such as the famous Camp Curry Firefall, which featured burning embers pushed off of a cliff) were necessities for the Yosemite tourist.[33]

While concessionaires usually did not raise the ire of park managers, the Yosemite Indians were still viewed with suspicion. The Yosemites, who continued to collect acorns in the valley after the parks were created, also generated income by providing fresh fish for campers and posing for tourists' photographs. Native women, in particular, were able to find jobs in hotels as domestics or selling baskets and crafts as souvenirs. Turn-of-the-century tourists viewed the valley's original inhabitants as quaint reminders of America's vanishing frontier past; park managers thought they were too unobtrusive to warrant their permanent banishment from the area.[34]

After the park service was founded, park officials experimented with a celebration of "Indian Field Days" for visitors' amusement. The Yosemites were paid to participate in rodeo competitions and wear headdresses, although neither were part of their culture. By the 1930s, park officials were pressuring the natives to leave the park, though restrictive labor, hunting, and land use regulations.[35] Native Americans were now viewed as an anachronism, or worse, a blight on Yosemite's wild, natural beauty. In contrast, few restrictions would be placed on the hordes of tourists that would continue to visit the park.

Middle- and upper-class travelers thus expected certain amenities when they visited the valley. Such distractions did not encourage tourists to view Yosemite as a natural area. Only a handful of hardy visitors strayed out of the narrow confines of the valley to experience the remote and "wild" areas of the park.

The failure of park officials to develop a comprehensive program for wildlife protection was highlighted by the park's chronic "bear problem." Early in the twentieth century, bears began to frequent hotel and campground garbage dumps, looking for food. The bears' nightly feedings soon became a draw for tourists, and eventually hotels began to feed the bears as part of a nightly show. Unfortunately, the bears often ransacked campers' food supplies, and occasionally bit or scratched visitors who were foolish enough to try to feed them by hand. Rather than assigning some of the blame for bad bear behavior to human beings, the park management dealt with these problems by relocating and occasionally killing bears. Furthermore, the widely held prejudice against predators encouraged national park officials to try to exterminate mountain lions and coyotes.[36]

The army superintendents and their men were vigilant in their efforts to protect Sequoia, Yosemite, and General Grant because they, like so many other Americans, had developed a great attachment to these national parks. According to Captain Dorst, "[t]he more one sees of [Sequoia,] the grander it seems. To despoil it would be a desecration."[37] The dedication of these men to protecting the parks from vandals and sheep helped insure that Americans would enjoy these grand California parks for years to come.

Nonetheless, dubious land management policies, such as complete fire suppression, would be reevaluated by future park managers. Heavy tourism in the valley during the summer months, overdevelopment of concessions, and the impact of wildlife management policies that focused, in part, on predator removal, would be long-term problems. Ironically, Yosemite's most efficient managers, the Yosemite Indians, no longer reside in the valley.

With the creation of these three California parks, Congress reaffirmed the monumentalism standard set by Yellowstone. Three parks established in the early twentieth century—Wind Cave, Sullys Hill, and Platt—did not seem to live up to this precedent.

FIVE

Natural Gems or Inferior Parks?
Wind Cave, Sullys Hill, and Platt

At the beginning of the twentieth century, the United States had five national parks that were celebrated for their unique and monumental features and their pristine natural beauty. Yellowstone, Yosemite, Sequoia, Mount Rainier, and Crater Lake are still considered by the American public to be some of the "gems" of the national park system. The three national parks that Congress established between 1902 and 1906—Wind Cave, Sullys Hill, and Platt—did not meet these high standards of grandeur and splendor, according to many park historians and critics.[1]

With the founding of Yellowstone, the federal government established the notion that a national park should have a breathtaking or strikingly unusual natural wonder that would appeal to visitors. Yellowstone and the other national parks were also expected to provide for the recreational wants of visitors. As the national park system grew, park superintendents began to include the protection of big game in the parks' mission. Although the concept of parks as wildlife preserves seemed to be at odds with visitors' recreation needs, the Department of the Interior and the superintendents of the parks struggled to strike a balance between developing the parks and protecting wildlife.

Ironically, big game and other animals often attracted tourists to the parks, which compounded the difficulties of wildlife protection.

As national parks, Wind Cave in South Dakota, Sullys Hill in North Dakota, and Platt in Oklahoma were expected to meet these vague, idiosyncratic, and conflicting standards. When they failed to measure up, they were criticized by park boosters and writers, and their park status was questioned by the Department of the Interior.

The National Park Service dealt with potentially inferior parks by "reshaping" them to fulfill park standards or terminating their national park status altogether. In the case of Wind Cave National Park, its major attraction, the cave itself, was viewed as somewhat less than monumental. The park service, however, promoted the park's undeveloped prairie lands and its wildlife preserve, which saved Wind Cave's park status. Sullys Hill and Platt, however, were not so lucky, and the park service eventually eliminated them from the ranks of the national parks. Sullys Hill had no unique natural feature, nor was it large enough to cater to the interests of recreation and wildlife preservation at the same time. As a result, it became a National Game Preserve in 1931. Although the park service maintained Platt's national park status for decades because it was politically expedient to do so, it ultimately became part of a national recreation area in 1978.

The National Park Service's treatment of these parks after 1916 illustrates the service's standards and its ability and willingness to adhere to them. It also highlights the importance national parks had gained as symbols of America's greatness by the early twentieth century.

The discovery of the cave that became the centerpiece of Wind Cave National Park is shrouded in the myth and folklore of the Black Hills. While Native Americans in the area probably knew about the cave for generations, local legend has credited a number of cowboys, outlaws, and explorers with finding the cave. Two hunters, Tom and Jesse Bingham, have been linked to the cave's "discovery" in 1881.[2] Although they may not have been the first white men to take notice of the cave, they sparked local interest in it that would culminate in the creation of a national park.

The Binghams found the cave because of a unique natural phenomenon—a strong breeze that blew in or out of the cave's only natural opening with changes in barometric pressure. As they passed the eighteen-inch opening to the cave, their hats blew off. After the Binghams showed the opening to a few friends, area interest in the cave began to grow. A few parties of adventurers from the nearby town of Hot Springs, South Dakota, did some initial exploration of the cave in the 1880s. Area residents called the cave "The Cave of the Winds" or "Wind Cave." By the late 1880s, the cave was consistently called "Wind Cave" in the local press.[3] As its existence became widely known, another party became interested in Wind Cave, for reasons other than its recreational value. The interested party was the South Dakota Mining Company.

In 1890, South Dakota Mining hired Jesse McDonald to manage its claim of Wind Cave. Although McDonald did not find valuable minerals in the cave, he did recognize the cave's aesthetic merits. McDonald and his family were soon developing and promoting the cave as a tourist attraction. The McDonalds built a tiny cabin over the mouth of the cave, explored the system extensively, named rooms and formations, and collected specimens that McDonald took to town to drum up interest in his new tourist attraction.

The family was soon guiding a steady stream of tourists through the cave. The tours were physically rigorous for visitors because there were no established paths or electric lights. The McDonalds, however, were not turning enough of a profit to support themselves, and Jesse therefore sold half of his interest in the cave to John Stabler, the manager of a hotel in Hot Springs. While the McDonalds and the Stablers staged a number of publicity stunts to promote the cave, it received truly national recognition from a collection of cave specimens that Jesse and his son Alvin displayed at the 1893 World's Fair in Chicago. The McDonalds' public relations triumph soon turned to tragedy, however, when Alvin died of typhus, which he contracted during the trip.[4]

After Alvin's death, the McDonalds, the Stablers, and the South Dakota Mining Company became locked in a legal battle for the cave. The McDonalds and the Stablers were dissatisfied with their partnership and tried to file separate claims on the cave and the land above it. Meanwhile, South Dakota Mining recognized the potential for profit from tourism and filed a claim on the cave's mineral rights.[5] Ironically, these legal maneuvers, combined with the national publicity that the McDonalds and the Stablers had generated for the cave, contributed to the eventual creation of a national park.

In 1898, after years of protracted litigation, two representatives of the U.S. Geological Survey were sent to assess the cave, particularly its size and attractiveness, to determine if it was worthy of national park status. Apparently, they were impressed with the cave's aesthetic merits. In their report, the surveyors did not hesitate to refer to formations and rooms by the names that the McDonalds had given them. They also took notice of the cave's unique geologic formations—boxwork—intersecting blades of calcium carbonate that have the appearance of post office mail slots, and frostwork—crystalline formations that cover the cave's walls like snow. The secretary of the interior did not recommend the creation of a national park in 1898, however, for the private claims had yet to be settled.[6]

By 1900, the federal government had ascertained that none of the parties contesting for control of Wind Cave had legitimate claims. No one had attempted to farm or mine the area, nor was there any indication that the area would be valuable for agriculture or mining in the future.[7] Without these claims blocking the way, the door was open for the federal government to create a national park.

The story might have been different, however, if Wind Cave had possessed valuable minerals, or the prairie above had been fertile farmland. The federal government had clearly established a precedent of founding national parks only in areas where the interests of lumbering, mining, or agriculture would not be jeopardized.[8] Congress traditionally had placed the interests of extractive industries over the ideal of aesthetic or wilderness conservation. As a result, Ferdinand V. Hayden of the Geologic Survey had to reassure a wary Congress in 1873 that Yellowstone was completely devoid of any industrial use before the first national park was created.[9] Likewise, Sequoia and General Grant National Parks would preserve only trees that were useless and inaccessible to lumbering interests. Mount Rainier National Park, founded in 1899, was established in an area too rugged to attract sheepherders or other commercial enterprises. Three years later, another remote park, Crater Lake, was established. As was the case for the other early parks, neither Mount Rainier nor Crater Lake received significant appropriations from Congress in their early years of existence.[10]

While Wind Cave clearly had merit as a tourist attraction that could economically benefit both its proprietor and the surrounding communities, Congress did not seem to value tourism as an industry. Apparently, in their view, only extractive industries served the nation as a whole. Thus, the nation could afford to preserve Wind Cave as a national park because it had been proven to be worthless to industry.

While Wind Cave's "worthlessness" paved the way for its future national park status, its reputation as a monumental national attraction was the main reason for reserving it. Congress set the standard for future national parks when it created Yellowstone to preserve curious geothermal phenomena, rather than a wilderness area. Eighteen years later, Congress created Sequoia and General Grant National Parks, which reserved the world's largest trees, and Yosemite, which would protect the magnificent Yosemite Valley as well as giant sequoias. Prior to Wind Cave's creation, Congress established national parks that would protect Washington's Mt. Rainier and the deepest lake in the United States, Oregon's Crater Lake. These parks were not meant to be representative wilderness areas. Thus, Wind Cave would have to possess an extraordinary or monumental attraction for it to obtain national park status.

Much of Wind Cave's value as a natural landmark rested on speculation that the cavern system might be the largest in the United States. In 1902, Mammoth Cave was the only standard for comparison. Wind Cave's reputation for expansiveness and unique natural beauty was enhanced when Special Agent M. A. Meyendorff of the Interior Department reported that he could offer Wind Cave "a second place to the Yellowstone . . . and declare the Wind Cave superior, in the point of attractiveness to the Mammoth Cave."[11] Meyendorff admired the cave's boxwork and geodes, lamented the damage done by specimen collectors, and speculated on the beauty of areas that had yet to be explored. With confirmation that the cave possessed scientific and aesthetic merit, and with speculation that it could be a truly monumental attraction, the Department of the Interior recommended Wind Cave for national park status.[12] No one was particularly concerned with preserving a representative sample of Dakota prairie land in this new park. Such lands would be set aside only because they were above a wonderful cave.

Representative William Lacey of Iowa spoke on behalf of the Wind Cave National Park proposal in Congress. A staunch supporter of national parks, Lacey informed his colleagues that the area "is substantially what the Yellowstone country would be if the geysers should die. . . . The active forces are no longer in operation . . . but a series of very wonderful caves remain."[13] While Lacey probably made this statement as a testament to the region's beauty, he may have reassured otherwise leery Congressmen that Wind Cave was as "worthless" as Yellowstone. In any case, the Wind Cave National Park Bill was passed quietly by both houses, and President Roosevelt signed the bill into law on 9 January 1903.

Soon after the new park's creation, a few critics suggested that Wind Cave was not worthy of national park status. Indeed, Secretary of the Interior Richard Ballinger voiced negative opinions of Wind Cave as early as 1910. Ballinger stated that Wind Cave could "never in any sense of the word become a [true] national park" because its "scenic attractiveness" was "not sufficient." He also believed that the cave was too remote to attract substantial numbers of visitors.[14]

Many other park critics and historians, past and present, have regarded Wind Cave as an "inferior" park. In the 1930s, Harlean James of the American Planning and Civic Association said that cave was "interesting" but should be a state park rather than a national park. Even Robert Sterling Yard of the National Parks Association dedicated only five sentences to Wind Cave in his 1919 *The Book of the National Parks,* a seemingly uncritical celebration of America's parks. Part of this criticism stemmed from the discovery that the cave was, in fact, smaller than Mammoth Cave.[15] In the 1920s, Carlsbad Caverns, the nation's largest cavern system, also received national recognition. With Wind Cave's reputation as a unique and monumental attraction devalued, park writers began to question its national park status.

Even though many park supporters criticized this national park, most believed that it was valuable enough to be preserved. After all, Wind Cave was a large system with unique boxwork and frostwork formations. The park was also located in the picturesque Black Hills, with Custer State Park, Jewel Cave, and the historic towns of Deadwood and Lead nearby. Nonetheless, some critics believed that scientific merit and pleasant surroundings did not equal the monumental requirements for national parks. From their perspective, national monument or state park status might have been more fitting for Wind Cave.

National monument status for Wind Cave was not an option, however, in 1903, because this designation for reserves was not created until 1906. The differences between the two designations are nebulous even today. The major difference is bureaucratic; Congress creates national parks, while the president establishes national monuments. Nonetheless, national parks traditionally are large reserves with monumental scenery and recreational opportunities, while national monuments preserve some particular archeological or natural feature.[16] If Wind Cave could not live up to the vague national park standards, it could probably meet the requirements for national monument status.

Although one of Wind Cave's critics charged that the park was a glorified "picnic site,"[17] the park could, and did, cater to a significant number of summer tourists. From 1903 to 1916, the park consistently attracted between three and four thousand visitors annually. While Yellowstone and Platt attracted far more tourists, Wind Cave's numbers compare favorably with Sequoia's, General Grant's, and Crater Lake's during the same period.[18]

Even though Wind Cave National Park received little funding prior to the creation of the National Park Service, this reflected the general pattern for congressional financing of national parks, rather than hostility toward Wind Cave in particular. Between 1902 and 1916, Wind Cave usually received twenty-five hundred dollars per year—a figure comparable to that given to Yosemite, Sequoia, and General Grant.[19] Many Congressmen clung to the idea that national parks could (and should) be self-supporting through admissions revenues and licensing fees for concessions, an idea that was first articulated when Yellowstone was created. Still others believed that the national parks did not need money for protection and development; simply setting aside lands for a park was enough.[20] As a result, the parks consistently received little funding from Congress.

While Wind Cave's annual appropriations were adequate to pay the superintendent's salary, maintain roads and the park's headquarters, impound stray cattle, and open new passageways in the cave itself, developments such as electric lamps for the cave and a new, more reliable water supply were delayed.[21] Nonetheless, the new park met the recreational wants of its visitors, including guided lamplight tours of the cave. The limits on public access may have protected the cave somewhat from specimen collectors. The McDonald and the Stabler children were some of the cave's first national park guides. Tourists could make a day trip to the park, or camp overnight.

The superintendent had the power to license concessionaires. Wagon and automobile tours from Hot Springs to the national park were the most common services. In 1913, the superintendent issued nine permits for these operations.[22] The fifty-dollar license fees augmented the park's meager congressional appropriations. Although there was not a great deal of demand for food service in the park, the first park superintendent, William A. Rankin, granted his own wife a permit to serve meals to tourists. Superintendent R. J. Pilcher also granted his wife a food service permit; she continued to furnish meals to Wind Cave visitors after his death in 1910.[23]

In 1912, the Department of the Interior enhanced Wind Cave's national park character by establishing a game preserve within the park's boundaries. With the introduction of bison and elk, Wind Cave National Park received a new tourist attraction. Superintendent Frederick N. Dille soon realized the bison's potential as an amusement for visitors, and suggested that a few animals should be penned "within a small inclosure [sic] alongside the road" for "the general public to obtain a glimpse."[24] While the cave itself might not have been a monumental attraction on the scale of the other national parks in the Interior Department's estimation, Wind Cave could now boast a wildlife preserve that added interest for park visitors.

The Department of the Interior's efforts to build up Wind Cave's national park character may have helped to preserve its national park status over the years. After the National Park Service was established in 1916, the national parks had a clearly defined mission to function as wildlife preserves. With bison and elk herds firmly established within the park's boundaries, Wind Cave seemed to fulfill adequately this preservation role.

In the end, Wind Cave's relative unworthiness as a national park was not based on an objective set of ecological standards; the cave simply did not measure up to the artificial standard of beauty or monumentalism set by the federal government. Wind Cave, after all, was deemed "inferior" partially because it paled in comparison to Mammoth Caves' or Carlsbad Caverns' size and grandeur. If these caves were to be the standard by which all other park proposals would be judged, then few caves in the United States could ever qualify for national park status.

Furthermore, the superintendents' and the Interior Department's attempts to make Wind Cave "worthy" through the addition of a wildlife preserve illustrate the limitations of national park wildlife protection and management policy. The government did provide protection for a limited number of buffalo and elk, but these were grazing animals that would appeal to park visitors. In this case, sightseeing took precedence over scientific considerations.

Wind Cave ultimately kept its national park status because it adequately fulfilled the requirements for at least recreation and wildlife. The cave was also an interesting, if not monumental, centerpiece for the park. In addition to extending the park's boundaries and officially embracing the wildlife preserve in the 1930s, the park service allowed prairie dogs to establish themselves in the park, thus creating one of the largest prairie dog towns in the country. Again, the park service was willing to accommodate an animal that would appeal to tourists. This policy was not based on environmental considerations.

The importance of wildlife as an attraction for Wind Cave National Park is reflected in many tourist guides and commentaries on the parks. Since the 1930s, guides and tour books have given equal weight to the "world of darkness" (the cave) and the "world of light" (the prairie and the animals).[25] Nearby attractions such as Custer State Park, Jewel Cave National Monument, and Mount Rushmore National Memorial have also added to Wind Cave National Park's appeal.

Thus, Wind Cave National Park was modified to fulfill general park standards that were eventually codified by the National Park Service. The park founded immediately after Wind Cave, Sullys Hill, could not be remade to fit these idiosyncratic standards. As a result, Sullys Hill did not retain its national park status.

Sullys Hill National Park has the dubious distinction of being the only national park that Congress did not purposefully create. The federal government received the 780 acres that comprised the Sullys Hill area from the

Devils Lake Sioux of the Fort Totten Reservation, North Dakota, by treaty on 27 April 1904. The agreement stipulated that the president could establish a public park on these grounds, and Theodore Roosevelt proclaimed the tract "Sullys Hill Park" on 2 June 1904.

Sullys Hill seems to have gotten its "national park" status by default. Clearly, it could not be a state or local park because the federal government controlled the area. While neither Congress nor the president called Sullys Hill a national park in 1902, it was treated as such by the Department of the Interior after that point. Indeed, Congress and the Interior Department seemed to use the titles "Sullys Hill Park" and "Sullys Hill National Park" interchangeably.

The strange birth of Sullys Hill National Park demonstrates clearly that the federal government lacked coherent procedures and standards for creating national parks. Nonetheless, Sullys Hill was not devoid of aesthetic attributes. Located on the south shore of Devils Lake, this reserve encompassed two miles of shoreline. The central topographical feature of this hilly, heavily forested park was the ridge known as Sullys Hill. The hill was the highest point in the park, and local myths and legends concerning its archeological and historical significance circulated widely. While these stories proved to be apocryphal, the park's superintendent boasted that the area's "natural beauties cannot be excelled."[26]

While Sullys Hill may have been a lovely natural area, it did not possess a monumental attraction that could be the centerpiece of a national park. The federal government, however, made every effort to find one. Immediately after the park was established, Congress appropriated five thousand dollars to the Interior Department to search for the fabled prehistoric Indian burial mounds and for valuable minerals. The survey failed to produce either.[27] This would be Congress's only expenditure on the park until 1914. Sullys Hill's lack of minerals probably saved its national park status in the short run; otherwise, the mining industry might have claimed the park in order to put the land to "productive" use.

Although Congress was notoriously stingy in its appropriations for national parks, its failure to provide any funding for the maintenance or protection of Sullys Hill is conspicuous. Members of Congress may have concluded that Sullys Hill was "inferior" to other national parks because it lacked a unique or monumental attraction, or they simply may have resented funding a park that they did not create. In any case, the park's acting superintendent's annual pleas for a permanent park guardian and money for development went unheeded.

When Sullys Hill National Park was established, the principal of the nearby Fort Totten Indian Industrial School, Charles M. Ziebach, was appointed acting superintendent for the park. Without federal funds or a staff, Ziebach did little more for the park than keep track of tourists and campers. Ziebach, however, did use his annual reports on the park's status from 1904 to 1916 to lobby for modest funding and a staff for the park. He argued that "by means of a small appropriation this park could be made one of the most beautiful and attractive spots in the State of North Dakota," and offered specific suggestions for development. [28] Ziebach wanted a dock within the park's limits for pleasure craft, and the removal of underbrush from the shoreline.[29] He also recommended the construction of a few bathhouses along the beach to accommodate visitors, for Sullys Hill offered "one of the best bathing places on Devil's Lake," in his estimation.[30] The park's most vocal supporter thus did not wish to maintain its "natural" state. Instead, he thought the park should be a tourist-oriented boating, swimming, and picnic site.

The superintendent noticed that visitors' enjoyment of the park was hampered by poor, undeveloped roads and trails that were virtually impassable after heavy rains. Requests for funding to improve these roads were therefore a regular feature of the superintendent's reports.[31] The construction of a guardian's headquarters and the clearing of picnic and camping grounds were also regular requests. Congress eventually followed only one of Ziebach's recommendations—the creation of a game preserve in the park. Ironically, the park's role in wildlife protection would ultimately eclipse its national park status.

In spite of the neglect, Sullys Hill did attract a fair number of visitors. In 1909, the park had approximately two hundred visitors, with forty of them camping for three days or more.[32] These visitors were both local picnickers and cross-country travelers who used the park as a rest stop. By 1914, annual visitors numbered approximately five hundred.[33]

In 1914, Congress appropriated five thousand dollars for what became Sullys Hill National Park's greatest attraction—a game preserve. These funds, however, did not go directly to the national park. Instead, the Biological Survey of the Department of Agriculture was charged with developing the reserve and constructing fences, corrals, and a headquarters.

The early definitions of game (or wildlife) preserves were as nebulous as those for the national parks and monuments. Using his ability to establish unilaterally national forests and monuments as a precedent, President Theodore Roosevelt created game and wildlife preserves to protect specific animals—usually birds or bison. Often, these early reserves did not have funding or a guardian, so private organizations, most notably the Audubon Society, would provide protection for the animals. Technically, the Agriculture Department was in charge of these reserves, whether or not private interests were involved in their management. Of course, efforts to protect America's most noble game animal, the bison, were supported by Roosevelt's fellow sportsmen. To a great extent, these game preserves shared the national parks' mission to protect symbols of America's grandeur and national heritage, but instead of protecting natural monuments, they protected distinctive animals. With pens and corrals for bison and other animals, Sullys Hill was a museum for animals—it did not necessarily protect natural habitat.

The herds of bison, elk, deer, and antelope that were cared for by the Agriculture Department proved popular with tourists at Sullys Hill. By 1930, the park was attracting approximately twenty thousand summer visitors. Acting Secretary of the Interior R. W. Dunlap noted that Sullys Hill was "an important recreational center for a large section of Minnesota and the Dakotas," and served the needs of "transcontinental travelers and other tourists" as well.[34]

Although the annual number of visitors to Sullys Hill continued to grow between 1904 and 1930, it still remained one of the least patronized parks. This was probably for the best, for the park was not big enough to maintain the wildlife preserve and cater to the recreational needs of a large number of visitors at the same time. Indeed, the park's meager picnic area and campgrounds were becoming overcrowded on Sundays and holidays in the later years of the park's life.[35]

The game preserve at Sullys Hill was critical to the park's future because it drew congressional funding and served as an attraction for visitors, thus giving the reserve more of a "national park" character. Unfortunately, Sullys Hill was too small to fulfill the national park roles of nature reserve, wildlife preserve, or recreational center. It also lacked the unique and monumental natural attraction that was embodied in most of the other national parks. As a result, the park would be officially turned over to the Department of Agriculture as a wildlife reserve in 1931.

The National Park Service, under the leadership of Horace Albright, pushed for the removal of Sullys Hill from the ranks of the national parks. Albright argued that the park had no scenery or attraction "that should entitle it to national-park status." Furthermore, the park was not being managed by the National Park Service because the national park had no funding. Only the game preserve, which was actively administered by the Biological

Survey of the Agriculture Department, received congressional funding.[36] Albright believed that the park's de facto game preserve status should be official; under his prompting, Congress officially endorsed Sullys Hill National Game Preserve.

Although most Americans would not have viewed such a small reserve as a "wilderness" area, it certainly had wild, untamed characteristics. This park's remoteness, combined with its lack of a monumental attraction, did not make it a leading national recreation center, and thus undermined its future park status.

The short life of Sullys Hill as a national park highlights the federal government's failure to define standards or procedures for the creation of parks before the park service was established in 1916. The development of general park standards by the National Park Service would lead to a reevaluation of all of the national parks, and to a change of official status for Sullys Hill. At this time the park service also began efforts to improve other "lesser" parks, such as Platt. In Platt's case, the park service found it politically expedient not to eliminate it from the ranks of the national parks. Thus, Platt would continue to be a national park until the late 1970s.

Of the fourteen parks in existence at the time the National Park Service was created, Platt was the only one whose status rested upon its reputation as a health resort.[37] This 780-acre reserve featured thirty-two mineral springs containing sulfur, bromide, and iron, and two freshwater springs. Throughout the twentieth century, Platt's visitors came to drink the waters and picnic by the park's springs. Platt did not, however, offer a monumental attraction, nor did it preserve a large tract of land or any significant variety of wildlife.

Located near the ancient Arbuckle Mountains in south-central Oklahoma, Platt was first visited by the Wichitas, Kiowas, and Comanches. Buffalo used the springs as a watering hole. Ironically, the first permanent residents in the Platt area were neither local Native Americans nor westward-migrating whites, but relocated Chickasaws and Choctaws, who began to use the future national park as a summer camping ground in the 1830s.[38]

By the turn of the century, however, whites had established a resort town near the springs, appropriately named Sulphur. The town provided food, lodging, and transportation for visitors who wanted to partake of the health benefits that mineral water supposedly offered. As the Indian Territory approached statehood and Sulphur grew, Native Americans became fearful that they would lose access to the springs. To prevent this, the Chickasaws and Choctaws sold the reserve to the federal government with the stipulation that the springs be maintained as a public reserve. Although the new Sulphur Springs Reserve had no official designation, it was placed in the care of the Department of the Interior.

In 1906, Connecticut's congressmen pushed to have the reserve formally designated "Platt National Park" in memory of Connecticut senator Orville Platt, who had been active in Indian affairs. This bill passed easily, probably because Congress was reassured that the establishment of the national park would require no additional outlay of funds.[39] Since Congress had already invested funds to purchase the reserve, establishment of a national park required only a change of title.

Most of Platt's visitors were area residents who came for the day to picnic, wade in the creeks, and enjoy its supposedly healing waters. Prior to the creation of the national park, concessionaires operated freely out of the town of Sulphur, providing surrey rides to and from the springs, food service within the reserve, and bottled spring water for sale. The area, therefore, was not economically "worthless" to the residents of Sulphur. This tiny reserve, however, embraced very little farmland or timber. It was useless to mining interests. Furthermore, Platt's national park status did not eliminate private enterprise in the area; any honest concessionaire could operate in the park as long as he paid the fifteen-dollar fee for a permit.[40]

Prior to the creation of the National Park Service, Platt generally received between five and ten thousand dollars per year from Congress. In 1909, the park received over twenty-two thousand dollars. Although these sums were not extravagant, they exceeded the funding for the California parks, Wind Cave, and Crater Lake for the same period.[41] Platt, however, was catering to more visitors than most of the other national parks. By 1916, Platt was the fourth-most frequently visited park, attracting between twenty-five thousand and thirty thousand visitors annually.[42] If nothing else, Platt was a recreational center.

The appropriations that Congress granted to the park paid the salaries of the superintendent, a ranger, a secretary, and two groundskeepers. The superintendent utilized the remaining funds for park development and improvements. These improvements included stone and suspension bridges, restrooms, paved roads, sidewalks, and pavilions over the springs. The superintendent also utilized federal funds to maintain the park's headquarters and lodging for himself and his staff. The rangers' duties included guarding the major bromide spring to ensure that tourists took only one gallon of water per visit.[43] While most of these improvements catered to visitors' comfort and enjoyment of the park, they certainly did not encourage visitors to look at Platt as a "natural" area. With these improvements, Platt began to look more like a planned city park than a national park like Yellowstone, Yosemite, or even tiny General Grant. General wilderness and wildlife preservation was not a goal at the park.

Some of the superintendents' other activities undermined Platt's natural qualities as well. One superintendent reported that he had sodded some areas of the park, while another boasted that he had planted alfalfa and corn in the park's open areas to feed the park's workhorses.[44] During a drought in 1911, the superintendent granted a permit to a local cattle rancher to use one of the springs as a watering hole for his livestock. For Platt's superintendents, profit potential, beautification projects, and the wants of tourists and area residents completely eclipsed preservation of the natural environment. From their reports to the Department of the Interior between 1906 and 1916, one gets the distinct impression that these men tried to groom, weed, beautify, or otherwise control most of the park's plant life. Of course, other parks' wildlife and natural resources were managed by human caretakers; Platt's lack of wilderness characteristics was just more obvious.

Unfortunately, Platt's main attraction was threatened by more than park improvements; encroaching urban development was also a great problem, as Sulphur's sewer occasionally contaminated the mineral springs. Sulphur's residents, Platt's superintendents, and Oklahoma's congressional representatives began to lobby for federal funding to rebuild the town's sewer system. In 1914, Congress granted $17,500 to correct the problem, with the stipulation that Sulphur provide matching funds.[45]

Although Platt catered to the recreational needs of the public, it could not match the monumentalism standard set by Yellowstone, Sequoia, and Yosemite. It was also too urbanized to be a natural refuge for big game. It could not even boast Hot Spring Reservation's spa image or Mackinac's historic attractions. The National Park Service, however, made an attempt to bring the park into line with these national park standards, and to make Platt the object of national pride.

The National Park Service made every effort to "improve" Platt and make it more worthy of its status. In 1920, the service established a herd of six bison in the park, creating another artificial wildlife reserve. During the 1930s, Civilian Conservation Corps projects included draining boggy areas, building new walkways, roads, bridges, and picnic areas, and digging out and lining the springs with native rock.[46] The park was also beautified with transplanted trees and other native Oklahoma flora. In later years, a veteran's hospital and an educational nature center were built in the park.

While these developments may have added to the public's appreciation for the park, most of these park projects further undermined the park's "natural character." Platt could never embody wilderness or the frontier the way the western parks could. It simply set aside a valuable resource.

In 1962, Congress established the Arbuckle National Recreational Area less than two miles away from Platt National Park. The centerpiece of the recreational area was the manmade Lake of the Arbuckles, which offered scuba diving, boating, swimming, and fishing to tourists. Visitors could also picnic, camp, and hunt in the surrounding hills. The new reserve was controlled by Platt's superintendent. Ironically, the Arbuckle National Recreational Area could serve the recreational wants of the public better than Platt, because it was larger and offered more activities to visitors. Nonetheless, Platt's springs and bison herd still drew tourists, and the nature center continued to serve as an educational resource. In 1978, Congress combined Arbuckle and Platt to form the Chickasaw National Recreation Area.

National recreation area status, at least superficially, seemed appropriate for Platt. National recreation areas were established at manmade lakes (or other areas where human tampering was obvious), so Americans could enjoy outdoor activities in a picturesque, albeit not wholly "natural," setting. Platt certainly could not boast "monumental" beauty, nor could it accommodate enough buffalo to be considered a game preserve. At least recreation area status endorsed Platt's recreational and educational functions.

Platt ultimately did not measure up to the park service's standards for national parks. It was not a wilderness area or a wildlife preserve. Its greatest asset was its springs, which attracted thirty thousand visitors annually. Platt's critics, however, argued that the springs were a regional attraction and not of national interest or importance. Although it could be argued that Yellowstone, Yosemite, and Sequoia attracted most of their visitors from western states, few critics attacked these parks for their regional appeal. Furthermore, Steven Mather and the park service would compromise on the "national significance" requirement for national parks if it were politically expedient to do so. Thus, Mather pushed for the creation of Acadia and Great Smoky Mountains National Parks, in part to garner more public support for national parks in the East. With Platt's "inferior" wildlife and national attractions, however, critics could use its regionalism as another angle of attack.

The major standards by which national parks are judged have changed very little since Wind Cave, Sullys Hill, and Platt were created. Nonetheless, the histories of these three parks demonstrate that the federal government lacked coherent standards and procedures for establishing national parks. The creation of these parks highlighted a need for an agency to evaluate park proposals and establish official standards for national parks. Under the Mather administration, the National Park Service outlined general criteria for national parks that embraced traditional but often unarticulated ideals for nature preservation, recreation, and monumentalism in national parks. Questions of utility, recreation, monumentalism, and wildlife preservation will continue to shape the destinies of the national parks. Often, the National Park Service's current standards seem inadequate to evaluate the parks' needs. In any case, Wind Cave, Sullys Hill, and Platt now have designations that, by the National Park Service's definitions, seem more appropriate.

In the end, Sullys Hill and Platt were deemed unsuitable to be national parks and were therefore "demoted" because they were not symbols of the nation's heritage, strength, or pride. While Yellowstone, Yosemite, and Sequoia preserved supreme natural monuments to the nation's greatness and protected the continent's noble game, these two "inferior" parks could boast only pleasant scenery, modest recreational opportunities, and limited wildlife protection. Sullys Hill was too small and Platt was too urbanized to share the responsibility of preserving an image (however distorted) of America's frontier, wilderness past with the other national parks. Wind Cave, however, did preserve uncultivated prairie lands and game, even though this was not the park's original mission. The cave was also a striking, if not unique, natural attraction that drew its share of tourists. Nonetheless, it is not one of the "crown jewel" parks that are most celebrated by Americans today.

SIX

"That Future Generations May Know the Majesty of the Earth"

The Establishment of the National Park Service, and Conclusions

At the beginning of the twentieth century, the War Department, the Interior Department, and the Agriculture Department all had interests in the national parks. While the army offered some protection for the national parks under its jurisdiction, its park stewardship could not last forever. In the nineteenth century, the army's intervention in the parks was a natural extension of the military's mission to pacify and "civilize" western frontier lands. As the army's role in the West decreased in the early twentieth century, however, so too did the War Department's interest in the national parks. Also, many of the conditions that had made military protection for the western parks necessary were reduced somewhat as time passed. Park area residents came to appreciate the tourist dollars that the reserves generated. Local support for the parks reduced some of the poaching and illegal grazing committed by park neighbors. In 1894, Congress allowed Wyoming law to be extended to cover Yellowstone, thus giving the area the legal protection it desperately needed. With these developments, some government officials and army officers claimed that civilians could now manage and protect the parks.

The Department of the Interior had a vested interest in bringing civilian management to all of the parks as well. For much of the nineteenth century, the army, under the direction of the secretary of the interior as well as the secretary of war, controlled all of the national parks. In the early twentieth century, however, the management of the America's national recreational lands and nature preserves became a bureaucratic nightmare. Of the twelve parks in existence in 1915, four—Yellowstone, Yosemite, Sequoia, and General Grant—were managed by the army. Civilian administrators provided some protection for the other parks. In addition, the Department of Agriculture controlled many of the national monuments through the Forest Service.

Because the Interior Department was now directly competing with the Agriculture Department for control of the public lands, the secretary of the interior actively lobbied Congress for the creation of a distinct parks bureau. As a result, the National Park Service of the Department of the Interior was born. Hereafter, national park management would be directed by this agency.

After forty years as the caretaker of some of America's most majestic and grandiose "curiosities," and twenty years after Mackinac was given to the State of Michigan, the army turned the national parks under its jurisdiction over to civilian administrators. Attempts to transfer these parks to civilian control had been made long before the National Park Service was created. President Theodore Roosevelt led the first campaign to remove the army from the western parks. After the Spanish-American War, Roosevelt feared that the United States was unprepared for a major military conflict.[1] He believed that the army should focus on military preparedness and professionalism. Roosevelt therefore argued that the army should be relieved of its nonmilitary duties to the national parks.

In 1907, Roosevelt appointed retired General S. B. M. Young to the position of superintendent of Yellowstone National Park. As superintendent, Young was to evaluate the park's future administrative needs and to formulate a plan for replacing the cavalry with civilian guardians. Young was an excellent choice for this mission. As a lieutenant colonel in the Fourth U.S. Cavalry, he acted as superintendent of Yellowstone after his distinguished service as superintendent of Yosemite National Park. Young was an enthusiastic administrator for both parks, and had a reputation for aggressively pursuing vandals and poachers.[2]

While Young was a loyal supporter of the parks, he believed that a civilian force could protect and manage the parks as effectively as the army did, and with less expense. Young estimated that the annual cost of a civilian administration, excluding the superintendent's salary, would be 50,000 dollars. In contrast, the military administration at Yellowstone cost over 150,000 dollars annually.[3] Young believed that former soldiers who had served in Yellowstone could be recruited into the civilian guard.

Nonetheless, Congress was not convinced that a civilian guard for the park could be cheaper than army troops. Also, Congress remembered the dismal record of the civilian superintendents that had served in Yellowstone prior to the army's intervention in the park. Congress therefore refused to act upon any of Young's recommendations.

The War Department's call to remove the army from national park duties was sounded again in 1911 when war broke out in Mexico. Secretary of War Henry L. Stimson believed that the army should prepare for possible expeditions into Mexico. With the approval of the secretary of the interior, Stimson called for a reduction in the number of men in Yellowstone and Yosemite, and for temporary removal of all troops from Sequoia and General Grant.[4]

The Interior Department now realized that it could not rely on the army to protect the "crown jewel" parks forever. As the administration of the parks became increasingly haphazard and unwieldy, the president called upon Congress to establish a national parks bureau.

Not surprisingly, the Department of the Interior wanted to control the new parks bureau; after all, it had ultimate responsibility and authority over the nature parks and some of the national monuments. The Forest Service of the Department of Agriculture, however, had opposed consistently the Interior Department's control of the national parks. Gifford Pinchot, who was instrumental in founding the Division of Forestry in 1898 and in upgrading it to bureau status in 1901, argued that the Forest Service should control the national parks. Pinchot reasoned that since many parks were heavily wooded "wilderness" areas, it made sense that a preexisting organization, dedicated to protection and management of forests (and some of the national monuments), should protect the national parks as well.[5]

Nonetheless, Pinchot and his Forest Service had a land management philosophy that was at odds with traditional park ideals. The Forest Service's primary mission, as Pinchot saw it, was to regulate the use of forests under its protection, not to preserve trees for their scenic value. Although Pinchot did appreciate beauty in nature, he was not willing to "waste" lumber resources by locking them up in an inviolable reserve. Instead, he believed that careful, scientific harvesting of trees would conserve this natural resource for future generations.[6]

This view, however, was not shared by an increasing number of park visitors. For nature enthusiasts, including Sierra Club members, the parks still were magnificent scenic preserves and monuments to nature's (and America's) grandeur. For many local concessionaires, parks provided a livelihood based on tourism. In any case, they argued, land that was truly "valuable" supposedly had been excluded from park boundaries in the first place.

The tensions between these two land management philosophies were highlighted when Woodrow Wilson, the Sierra Club, and the city of San Francisco became locked in a battle over the Hetch Hetchy Valley in Yosemite National Park. The Hetch Hetchy Valley's reputation for natural beauty and majesty rivaled that of the Yosemite Valley itself. As early as 1882, however, San Francisco had wanted to dam the valley to provide a consistent water supply for the city. The city's request became more urgent after the great earthquake and fire of 1906. In 1913, Wilson, who owed his election, in part, to the state of California, was willing to listen to the city's pleas.[7]

In spite of America's tradition of placing nature's utility over aesthetics, the Sierra Club, the Appalachian Mountain Clubs, and many women's organizations rallied to Hetch Hetchy's defense. John Muir and Robert Underwood Johnson led this unprecedented campaign for conservation. Although a flurry of sympathetic magazine articles, pro-Hetch Hetchy advertising, and letters to senators failed to save the valley from the dam project, this mass mobilization of park supporters signaled a pronounced shift from America's early-nineteenth-century hostility towards wild areas. As Roderick Nash has noted, even supporters of the dam argued that the preservation of scenery was a noble goal; they insisted that, in this case, human needs outweighed the aesthetic value of the valley. Indeed, a few of the project's advocates maintained that the dam would enhance Hetch Hetchy's beauty as well as the recreational opportunities in Yosemite National Park.[8]

After suffering through the controversy surrounding the Hetch Hetchy Dam project, Congress was not as willing to side with the "utilitarian" interests of the Forest Service in the national park bureau debate. In 1916, Congress passed the Park Service Bill, and Steven Mather became the head of the National Park Service. Mather's new agency was charged with conserving "the scenery and the natural and historic objects and the wildlife" of the reserves. At the same time, the park service was supposed to provide for public "enjoyment" of the parks while leaving the natural attractions "unimpaired for the enjoyment of future generations."[9]

A man of boundless energy and dedication to the national parks, Steven Mather was well suited to the directorship of the park service. Mather, a millionaire who had made his fortune in borax, also had the prestige needed to garner political support for the parks. Often he would finance park projects with his own money.[10]

As director of the National Park Service, Mather controlled the Hot Springs Reserve, the national monuments that already were protected by the Interior Department, and all of the national parks. The national forests and the monuments that were managed by the Forest Service remained under the control of the Department of Agriculture. The army continued to care for the national historic battlefield sites. Thus, agency rivalries were not completely eliminated with the creation of the new agency. These problems would not be resolved until the 1930s, when the National Park Service, under the leadership of Horace T. Albright, gained control of the national historic battlefields and all of the national monuments.[11]

Mather and the secretary of the interior quickly established general missions for the national parks that the park service and most Americans subscribe to today. The parks were to "preserve . . . in essentially [its] natural state . . . scenery of supreme and distinctive quality or some natural feature so extraordinary or unique as to be of national interest and importance." Mather argued that the new park service also should encourage recreational use of the parks by increasing automobile access, developing interpretive and educational programs, and working with concessionaires on park improvements.[12]

Mather believed that mass public support for the parks was critical for his agency's—and the park system's—survival. Thus, he made road development, improved concessions, and increased park visitation top priorities. To generate more eastern support for the park service and to make national parks more accessible to people who could not travel long distances, Mather pushed for the inclusion of Acadia, Shenandoah, and Great Smoky Mountains National Parks in the new system. Predictably, Robert Sterling Yard, head of the National Parks Association, was dismayed at the inclusion of Shenandoah in the system, for it did not meet the high standards for wilderness, beauty, and grandeur set by the other early parks, in his estimation.[13] Thus, problems of monumentalism, national significance, and balancing recreation and environmental protection would continue to plague the park system and its administrators even after the creation of the National Park Service.

Interestingly, the lean years of the Great Depression would mark a period of tremendous growth and development for the national park system. In an effort to streamline environmental management, the federal government turned all of the national monuments and battlefields over to the National Park Service in 1933. Along with this expansion in the park system's holdings, the Civilian Conservation Corps, one of the Roosevelt administration's "make-work" programs, built roads, bridges, and visitors' centers, and generally improved the parks' physical facilities.[14] Such developments in the park system's infrastructure, however, did not help protect park ecosystems or natural attractions.

Construction and physical improvement in the parks was emphasized again after World War II. After years of financial neglect during the war, a massive campaign was launched in 1956 to improve visitor access to the parks. Known as Mission 66, this ten-year project to improve and restore neglected park facilities was largely successful, but did little to foster wildlife protection or to encourage the public's appreciation of wild lands.

In spite of the emphasis on development in the parks during this period, the National Park Service was also developing an increased interest in the protection of the ecosystems contained in the parks. By 1963, one of the park service's goals was "managing the national parks and monuments . . . to preserve, or where necessary to recreate, the ecologic scene as viewed by the first European visitors." By working to protect an ecosystem, the service could make a national park "represent a vignette of primitive America."[15]

In June and July 1962, the first World Conference on National Parks was held in Seattle, Washington. One hundred forty-five delegates, representing sixty-three different countries, and 117 representatives from individual states of America gathered to discuss general park standards and ideals, the economic and cultural benefits of national parks, international environmental problems, biological research, endangered wildlife, and management of parks and natural resources. Days before the conference began, President John F. Kennedy sent a letter of welcome to each of the delegates. In this letter, Kennedy presented a view of the national parks that would not have been wholly unfamiliar to late-nineteenth-century Americans. Kennedy argued that the parks offered "release from the tension of an increasingly industrialized civilization" through "personal contact with the natural environment."

The parks, in his estimation, should preserve "outstanding scenic and scientific assets" as well as "magnificent and varied wildlife." By setting aside "an ample portion of our national resources as national parks and reserves" today, "future generations" could "know the majesty of the earth."[16]

Recently, international conferences have clarified the scientific mission of the national parks. Ideally, national parks should be large enough to preserve representative samples of a nation's ecosystems and indigenous plants and animals. Nonetheless, parks are also tourist attractions and scenic monuments. Thus, the American model for national parks has been quite influential.[17]

Although America's park guardians and most park visitors accept the early park standards for scenic preservation, recreation, and wildlife protection, the problems and contradictions inherent to these standards have not lessened with the passage of time. With overcrowding in popular parks such as Yosemite, modern tourism in the national parks undermines the park service's mission to preserve the parks in a pristine state. Urban problems such as pollution and high population density in peak travel months impugn the image of parks as wilderness or an escape from the pressures of modern-day life.

Today's critics of the National Park Service's development and visitor policies argue that the service has placed travelers' comfort and convenience over wildlife protection. Joseph Sax has argued that the park service should limit construction in the parks, and encourage "reflective" or "contemplative" recreation, such as hiking and horseback riding. Although he recognizes the need to provide access for visitors with physical disabilities, Sax argues that many projects intended to make parks easily accessible, such as road construction and sightseeing trams, actually limit a visitor's ability to fully appreciate and enjoy the parks' natural beauty.[18]

Although misuse and overdevelopment may do irreparable damage to the parks, the willingness of park service employees and Congress to deem some parks "inferior" may do even more harm to the system. It is easy to justify the existence of "crown jewel" parks that are older, are more famous, and boast superlative natural attractions; it is far more difficult to prove that Wind Cave or Hot Springs are "worthy" members of the world's first park system. According to Dwight F. Rettie, the cult of the crown jewel parks makes other valuable but lesser-known areas vulnerable to decommissioning because of political whim. It also endangers funding for newer, smaller parks, and exacerbates overcrowding in popular parks. Rettie argues that these supposedly inferior parks often attract substantial numbers of visitors and are very important regional education and recreation areas.[19] Nevertheless, many park proposals have been labeled "park barrel" legislation because new park designations are being exploited for the tourist dollars they can bring to a region.[20]

Clearly, the seeds of the American park system were sown with the creation of Hot Springs Reservation. Congress's impulse to preserve these supposedly healing waters was inspired, in part, by Europe's luxury spas. Congress also wished to avoid the national embarrassment spawned by the crass exploitation of another natural tourist attraction, Niagara Falls. Thus, nature preservation in the United States was born of cultural insecurity and sensitivity to European criticism of American tastes.

American architecture and cultural achievements, however, could not rival the grandeur or antiquity of Europe's. Nevertheless, the young nation did have monumental natural attractions that could match, and even surpass, anything that Europe could offer. The natural curiosities and spectacular vistas of the early western parks, such as Yellowstone, Yosemite, and Sequoia, were a source of national pride.

For a small contingent of nineteenth-century travelers, nature lovers, intellectuals, and sportsmen, the national parks also were the last remnants of the country's pioneer past. These park defenders feared that such frontier virtues as strength, stamina, self-reliance, and morality were slipping away from urban Americans. Such concerns became more acute at the turn of the century, when it became apparent that America's wild "frontier" lands were disappearing. Thus, national parks afforded middle- and upper-class urban American travelers the opportunity to have contact with the untamed "wilderness" of early America—but in a controlled, managed environment.

These samples of "wilderness" were protected and developed by both civilian and army managers. These human caretakers protected animals that would appeal to tourists, drove domestic animals away from the reserves, built roads and trails, cleared brush, fought fires, and monitored concessionaires (who provided for visitors' "needs"). Park managers also attempted to limit Native Americans' access to the parks, believing that Indians made the parks too wild or were a threat to these managed, "natural" areas. In any case, park superintendents did not protect pristine, frontier lands, but natural museums that were dedicated to preserving America's pioneer past.

Tiny Mackinac Island fulfilled this museum role as well as the other early parks, and it certainly was a popular travel destination. Mackinac's visitors could enjoy both the pioneer spirit and the amenities of a luxury resort and spa. Visitor interest in the island's fort foreshadowed the National Park Service's role in historic preservation. The decommissioning of Mackinac National Park also underscores the fragility of the park system as a whole. Thus, the short-lived Mackinac National Park may be as important to understanding Americans' expectations for such reserves as are Yellowstone or Yosemite.

As the nation contemplates the future of its national parks at the beginning of the twenty-first century, it will have to confront the difficulties of establishing, funding, and developing national parks—problems that park supporters faced at the dawn of the twentieth century. The wilderness ideal and the "Worthless Lands Thesis" are still factors in park service planning, as demonstrated by the high concentration of parks in the West and Alaska. These issues will become even more critical as opportunities to experience nature in a nonurban setting diminish. While the U.S. National Parks do stand as monuments to the wonder of nature and the country's frontier past, so, too, do they illustrate the limitations of the nation's conservation and preservation policies.

NOTES

INTRODUCTION

1. Roderick Nash, *Wilderness and the American Mind* (New Haven, Conn.: Yale University Press, 1967).

2. Ibid., 47.

3. William Cronon, "Introduction: In Search of Nature," in *Uncommon Ground: Rethinking the Human Place in Nature* (New York: W.W. Norton & Company, 1996), 23–56.

4. Robert Pogue Harrison, *Forests: The Shadow of Civilization* (Chicago: University of Chicago Press, 1992), 247.

5. H. Duane Hampton, "Opposition to National Parks," *Journal of Forest History* 25 (January 1981): 42.

6. Alfred Runte, "'Worthless' Lands—Our National Parks," *American West* 15 (May 1973): 4–11. The "worthless lands thesis" is also a major theme in Runte's survey of U.S. park history, *National Parks: The American Experience,* 3d ed. (Lincoln: University of Nebraska Press, 1997).

7. John Ise, *Our National Park Policy: A Critical History* (Baltimore: Johns Hopkins University Press, 1961).

8. H. Duane Hampton, *How the U.S. Cavalry Saved Our National Parks* (Bloomington: Indiana University Press, 1971). Harvey Meyerson has examined the Fourth U.S. Cavalry's role in protecting Yosemite National Park in *Nature's Army: When Soldiers Fought for Yosemite* (Lawrence: University Press of Kansas, 2001). While Meyerson does an excellent job of placing the army's mission in the national parks in the larger context of nineteenth-century American military history, he does not examine the long-term impact of some of the army's environmental management policies.

CHAPTER 1

1. One of the most striking examples is John Ise's *Our National Park Policy* (Baltimore: Johns Hopkins University Press, 1961). Although Ise dedicates large sections of his book to the earliest national parks, he offers only a cursory treatment of Hot Springs, and dismisses it as "not scenically important" (13).

2. M. S. Bedinger, *Valley of the Vapors: Hot Springs National Park* (Philadelphia: Eastern National Park and Monument Association, 1974), 8.

3. John C. Paige and Laura Soulliere Harrison, *Out of the Vapors: A Social and Architectural History of Bathhouse Row: Hot Springs National Park, Arkansas* (Washington, D.C.: U.S. Department of the Interior, 1988), 22.

4. Wayne Fields, "The Double Life of Hot Springs," *American Heritage* 42 (April 1991): 108.

5. Bedinger, *Valley of the Vapors,* 13.

6. Paige and Harrison, *Out of the Vapors,* 32.

7. John Shultis, "Improving the Wilderness: Common Factors in Creating National Parks and Equivalent Reserves during the Nineteenth Century," *Forest and Conservation History* 39 (July 1995): 121–22.

8. Alfred Runte, *National Parks: The American Experience,* 3d ed. (Lincoln: University of Nebraska Press, 1997), 2–4.

9. Ibid., 5–6; Anne Whiston Spirn, "Constructing Nature: The Legacy of Frederick Law Olmsted," in *Uncommon Ground,* 95–96; Shultis, "Improving the Wilderness," 122. Niagara Falls became a state park in the late nineteenth century.

10. Foster Rhea Dulles, *A History of Recreation: America Learns to Play* (New York: Meredith Publishing Company, 1965), 149–51. See also Ronald F. Lee, *Family Tree of the National Park System* (Philadelphia: Eastern National Park and Monument Association, 1974), 15–16, and Barry Mackintosh, *The National Parks: Shaping the System* (Washington, D.C.: National Park Service, 1985), 15.

11. Dulles, *History of Recreation,* 149.

12. Fields, "Double Life," 107.

13. Ibid., 110.

14. Paige and Harrison, *Out of the Vapors,* 47.

15. Ibid., 77.

16. *Report of the Superintendent of the Hot Springs Reservation to the Secretary of the Interior* (Washington, D.C.: Government Printing Office, 1899), 4, 8, 11–13.

17. Fields, "Double Life," 111. See also Patricia L. Hudson, "Taking the Waters in Style," *Americana* 18 (January/February 1991): 46.

18. Fields, "Double Life," 110.

19. *Fordyce Bath House: Arkansas Hot Springs* (Hot Springs, Ark.: n.p., n.d.), 4.

20. Opie Read, foreword to *Hot Springs National Park, Arkansas,* by L. M. Allen (Hot Springs, Ark.: Rock Island Lines, 1922), 4–5.

21. Ibid., 5, and *Legend of the Quapaw Baths* (reprint, Hot Springs: National Park Service, 1984), 9.

22. For example, L. M. Allen, in *Hot Springs National Park,* suggests that "the fame of these hot springs" may have "first prompted Ponce de Leon to embark upon his romantic search for the fountain of eternal youth." He does concede, however, that de Soto was more likely to have visited the springs than de Leon (6). The *Legend of the Quapaw Baths* states that de Soto believed he had found the "Fountain of Youth" (4). The author of

Fordyce Bath House also connects the legend of the fountain of youth with de Soto, and implies that de Soto died because he had a "disease which only gold could cure" (4).

23. Edwina Walls, "The Public Health Service VD Clinic in Hot Springs, AR," *Public Health Reports* 110 (January/February 1995): 103.

24. For example, see Robert Sterling Yard, *The Book of the National Parks* (New York: Charles Scribner's Sons, 1919), 308; *Fordyce Bath House*, 6; Allen, *Hot Springs National Park*, 11.

25. Department of the Interior, *General Information Regarding the Hot Springs of Arkansas* (Washington, D.C.: Government Printing Office, 1912), 8–9.

26. By 1916, Hot Springs was attracting 118,740 visitors annually, while Yellowstone drew only 35,849. See Ronald A. Foresta, *America's National Parks and Their Keepers* (Washington, D.C.: Resources for the Future, Inc., 1984), 11–12.

27. Runte, *National Parks*, 132, 217–18, and Thomas A. Wikle, "Proposals, Abolishments, and Changing Standards for U.S. National Parks," *Historian* 54 (autumn 1991): 50–51.

28. Kay Danielson, "Hot Springs Revival," *National Parks* 62 (September/October 1988): 33–34.

29. Margaret F. Boorstein, "The Wonders and Origins of Four National Parks of the Southern United States," *Focus* 42 (winter 1992): 27, and Fields, "Double Life," 115.

CHAPTER 2

1. Alfred Runte, *National Parks: The American Experience*, 3d ed. (Lincoln: University of Nebraska Press, 1997), 42.

2. Ronald F. Lee, *Family Tree of the National Park System* (Philadelphia: Eastern National Park and Monument Association, 1974), 9.

3. Dyan Zaslowsky, *These American Lands: Parks, Wilderness and the Public Lands* (New York: Henry Holt and Company, 1986), 10. Zaslowsky argues that the earliest parks served a basic, yet "revolutionary purpose of preserving spectacular landscapes for the pleasure of the public."

4. Katherine E. Early, *"For the Benefit and Enjoyment of the People": Cultural Attitudes and the Establishment of Yellowstone National Park* (Washington, D.C.: Georgetown University Press, 1984), 10; Nathaniel Pitt Langford, *Diary of the Washburn Expedition to the Yellowstone and Firehole Rivers in the Year 1870* (St. Paul, Minn.: F. J. Haynes Co., 1905), xxxi; and Zaslowsky, *These American Lands*, 14. See also Audrey L Haines, *The Yellowstone Story: A History of Our First National Park* (Denver: Colorado Associated University Press, 1977), 1:53–59. Haines argues that many of the tall tales attributed to Bridger are more recent inventions.

5. Paul A. Hutton, "Phil Sheridan's Crusade for Yellowstone," *American History Illustrated* 19 (February 1985): 11.

6. David E. Folsom, "The Folsom-Cook Exploration of the Upper Yellowstone in the Year 1869," with an introduction by N. P. Langford, in *Contributions to the Historical*

Society of Montana, vol. 5, (Boston: J. S. Canner and Company, Inc., 1966), 364–69. For other discussions of this expedition, see Early, *"For the Benefit and Enjoyment of the People,"* 15; Harlean James, *Romance of the National Parks* (New York: Macmillan Company, 1939), 16; Lee, *Family Tree,* 11–12; Barry Mackintosh, *The National Parks: Shaping the System* (Washington, D.C.: National Park Service, 1985), 12; Irving R. Melbo, *Our Country's National Parks* (Indianapolis: Bobbs-Merril Company, 1941), 1:6–7; and John Reiger, *American Sportsmen and the Origins of Conservation,* rev. ed. (Norman: University of Oklahoma Press, 1986), 95. Alfred Runte argues that Langford's account of the group's decision to advocate the creation of a "national" park is highly idealized. See *National Parks,* 41–42.

7. See T. C. Everts, "Thirty-Seven Days of Peril," *Scribner's Magazine* (November 1871), in *Contributions to the Historical Society of Montana* (Boston: J. S. Canner and Company, Inc., 1966), 5: 349–69.

8. U.S. Senate, Senator Pomeroy of Kansas speaking for the Resolution to Set Apart the Yellowstone Region as a National Park, 42d Cong., 2d sess., *Congressional Globe* (22 January 1872), 171, pt. 1: 697.

9. Ibid.

10. Ibid.

11. See Roderick Nash, *Wilderness and the American Mind* (New Haven, Conn.: Yale University Press, 1967), 110–12, and Early, *"For the Benefit and Enjoyment of the People,"* 7.

12. Paul Herman Buck, *The Evolution of the National Park System of the United States* (Washington, D.C.: Government Printing Office, 1946), 11.

13. U.S. Senate, Senator Pomeroy 697; and U.S. House, Delegate Claggett of Montana speaking for the Resolution to Establish a Public Park on the Yellowstone River, 42d Cong., 2d sess., *Congressional Globe* (27 February 1872), 172, pt. 1: 1243–44.

14. Hiram Martin Chittenden, *The Yellowstone National Park: Historical and Descriptive,* 4th ed. (Cincinnati: Robert Clarke Company, 1933), 104.

15. "It was, perhaps, during this period that Langford's friends suggested that his initials N.P. stood for 'National Park,' and he sometimes wrote in the Spencerian script of the day, 'National Park' Langford." (James, *Romance,* 18).

16. As late as 1916, Hot Springs was attracting 118,740 visitors annually, while Yellowstone drew only 35,849. See Ronald A. Foresta, *National Parks and Their Keepers,* (Washington, D.C.: Resources for the Future, Inc., 1984), 11–12. Indeed, Hot Springs was the most frequently visited reserve until 1925. See Earl Pomeroy, *In Search of the Golden West: The Tourist in Western America* (New York: Alfred A. Knopf, 1957), 119.

17. See Nash, *Wilderness,* 108.

18. Rudyard Kipling, *American Notes* (Boston: Brown and Company, 1899), 75–76, 79; Pomeroy, *Golden West,* 53–54, 59, 92; Edwards Roberts, *Shoshone and Other Western Wonders* (New York: Harper & Brothers, 1888), 202.

19. For a discussion of this general problem, see Paul Andrew Mogren, "The Development of a Philosophy of Land Reservation on General Land Office, United States For-

est Service, and National Park Service Lands, 1787 to 1947" (Ph.D. diss., University of Utah, 1980), 54.

20. H. Duane Hampton, *How the U.S. Cavalry Saved Our National Parks* (Blooming-ton: Indiana University Press, 1971), 61.

21. Hutton, "Sheridan's Crusade,"12.

22. Buck, *Evolution of the National Park System*, 23–24.

23. Mark Spence, "Dispossessing the Wilderness: Yosemite Indians and the National Park Ideal, 1864–1930," *Pacific Historical Review* 65 (February 1996): 39.

24. Ibid., 39–40n. 38. Writers who have argued that Indians did not use park lands include Hiram Chittenden (*Yellowstone National Park*, 11–12), Paul Herman Buck (*Evolution of the National Park System*, 3n. 1), and Stuart Sherman White ("The National Parks—100 Years Later: A Photojournalist's Study of the Changing Philosophy of the National Parks System, Observed and Photographed in Yellowstone" [master's thesis, Kent State University, 1973], 11–12). Although Chittenden, Buck, and White (who relies heavily on Chittenden and Buck as sources) do not accept Norris's geyser story, they do assume that the Indians did not frequent the area because the park lands were useless to them. See also James, *Romance*, 1–2.

25. Spence, "Dispossessing the Wilderness," 38–39. Spence notes that Alfred Runte's "Worthless Lands" thesis applies only to whites' views of the Yellowstone area (39 n. 38).

26. Hutton, "Sheridan's Crusade," 12.

27. Hampton, *U.S. Cavalry*, 62–69.

28. U.S. House, *Indians and Yellowstone Park*, report to the Special House Commit-tee on Indian Education and Yellowstone National Park, 49th Cong., 1st sess., 1885, H.R. 1076, microfiche, 63.

29. Hampton, *U.S. Cavalry*, 73.

30. John Ise, *Our National Park Policy*, (Baltimore: Johns Hopkins University Press, 1961), 36–37, 44.

31. U.S. House, *Annual Report of the Superintendent of Yellowstone National Park, 1886*, 49th Cong., 2d sess., 1886, Ex. Doc. 1, microfiche, 1076.

32. Spence, "Dispossessing the Wilderness," 40.

33. U.S. House, *Annual Report of the Superintendent of Yellowstone National Park, 1891*, 51st Cong., 2d sess., 1891, Ex. Doc. 1, microfiche, 645.

34. See Reiger, *American Sportsmen*, 98–113.

35. Ibid., 104.

36. Ibid., 100–101, 104.

37. U.S. House, *Annual Report of the Superintendent of Yellowstone National Park, 1887*, 50th Cong., 2d sess., 1887, Ex. Doc. 1, microfiche, 1300; and John F. Berber, *Old Yellowstone Views* (Missoula, Mont.: Mountain Press Publishing Company, 1987), 33.

38. U.S. House, *Annual Report of the Superintendent of Yellowstone National Park, 1890*, 52d Cong., 2d sess., 1890, Ex. Doc. 1, microfiche, 351.

39. Ibid., 353.

40. U.S. House, *Annual Report of the Superintendent, 1887,* 1302.

41. Ibid.

CHAPTER 3

1. For example, Alfred Runte mentions Mackinac only in passing, stating that "it hardly qualified as a scenic wonderland" (*National Parks: The American Experience,* 3d ed. [Lincoln: University of Nebraska Press, 1997], 53). Ronald Foresta (*National Parks and Their Keepers* [Washington, D.C.: Resources for the Future, Inc., 1984], 16), Dyan Zaslowsky (*These American Lands: Parks, Wilderness and the Public Lands* [New York: Henry Holt and Company, 1986], 18), and Joseph L. Sax (*Mountains without Handrails: Reflections on the National Parks* [Ann Arbor: University of Michigan Press, 1980], 6) only note the park's existence. Harlean James's *Romance of the National Parks* (New York: Macmillan Company, 1939) does not say anything about the park, nor does Freeman Tilden's *The National Parks* (New York: Alfred A. Knopf, 1986). Surprisingly, Duane Hampton's *How the U.S. Cavalry Saved Our National Parks* (Bloomington: Indiana University Press, 1971) treats Mackinac with only an extended footnote, even though this study focuses on the army's ties to the national parks (221 n. 83.) John Ise (*Our National Park Policy* [Baltimore: Johns Hopkins University Press, 1961]) dismisses the park in two pages as a "rich man's summer resort" (49) that "never amounted to much" (55). Keith R. Widder's *Mackinac National Park: 1875–1895* (Williamston, Mich.: TriKraft, Inc., 1975) provides an extensive, although relatively uncritical, overview of the park's history. Widder's work offers no comparison between Mackinac and the other early national parks. See also Kathy S. Mason, "The Gem of the Straits: Mackinac 1875–1895," *Inland Seas* 49 (winter 1993): 246–58.

2. See Keith R. Widder, *Reveille Till Taps: Soldier Life at Fort Mackinac, 1780–1895* (Lansing, Mich.: TriKraft, Inc., 1972), 28–35.

3. See Alexander Henry, *Attack at Michilimackinac: Alexander Henry's Travels and Adventures in Canada and the Indian Territories Between the Years 1760 and 1764,* ed. David A. Armour (Lansing, Mich.: TriKraft, Inc., 1971), 73, for a discussion of the Skull Cave legend.

4. U.S. Senate, Senator Ferry of Michigan speaking for the Resolution Directing the Secretary of War to Consider the Expediency of Dedicating to the Public Use So Much of the Island of Mackinac Now Held by the United States, 43d Cong., special sess., *Congressional Record* (11 March 1873), 1, pt.1:39.

5. Walter Havighurst, *Three Flags at the Straits: The Forts at Mackinac* (Englewood Cliffs, N.J.: Prentice-Hall, 1966), 185.

6. U.S. Senate, Ferry, Resolution Directing the Secretary of War, 39.

7. Ibid., 40.

8. Ibid., 41.

9. Ibid.

10. U.S. Senate, *Information in Relation to the Expediency of Dedicating to the Public Use Part of the Island of Mackinac,* 43d Cong., 1st sess., 1873, Ex. Doc. 28, microfiche, 3.

11. U.S. House, Representative Conger of Michigan speaking for the Resolution to Set Apart a Certain Portion of the Island of Mackinac as a National Park, 43d Cong., 2d sess., *Congressional Record* (3 March 1875), 1, pt. 3:2242.

12. Havighurst, *Three Flags,* 185–89.

13. U.S. Senate, Senator Ferry of Michigan speaking for the Resolution to Set Apart a Certain Portion of the Island of Mackinac as a National Park, S. No. 28, 43d Cong., 1st sess., *Congressional Record* (28 May 1874), 2, pt. 5:4322.

14. Runte, *National Parks,* 56.

15. Earl Pomeroy, *In Search of the Golden West: The Tourist in Western America* (New York: Alfred A. Knopf, 1957), 43.

16. Roderick Nash, *Wilderness and the American Mind* (New Haven, Conn.: Yale University Press. 1967), 104.

17. Ibid., 90–95.

18. Angie Bingham, "Devil's Kitchen, Mackinaw Island," in *Collections and Researches Made by the Michigan Pioneer and Historical Society* (Madison, Wis.: Democrat Printing Co., 1898), 14:336; Dwight H. Kelton, *Annals of Fort Mackinac* (Detroit: Detroit Free Press Printing Co., 1894), 8; Meade C. Williams, *Early Mackinac: A Sketch, Historical and Descriptive* (St. Louis: Buchart Bros., 1897), 139; Constance Fenimore Woolson, "'Fairy Island' As Seen by Constance Fenimore Woolson," in *Historic Mackinac: The Historical, Picturesque and Legendary Features of the Mackinac Country,* ed. Edwin Orin Wood (New York: Macmillan Company, 1918), 407.

19. "Mackinac," from the *New York Tribune,* 1859, in *Report of the Pioneer Society of the State of Michigan* (Lansing, Mich.: Thorp and Godfrey, 1886), 7:201–2.

20. Foster Rhea Dulles, *A History of Recreation: America Learns to Play* (New York: Meredith Publishing Company, 1965), 149.

21. J. A. Van Fleet, *Old and New Mackinac: With Copious Extracts from Marquette, Hennepin, La Hontan, Alexander Henry, and Others* (Grand Rapids, Mich.: "The Lever" Book and Job Office, 1880), 146.

22. John R. Bailey, *Mackinac, Formerly Michilimackinac: A History and Guide Book with Maps* (Grand Rapids, Mich.: Tradesman Company, 1895), 221.

23. Henry R. Schoolcraft, *Personal Memoir of a Residence of Thirty Years with the Indian Tribes on the American Frontiers* (Philadelphia: Lippincott, Gramo, and Co., 1851), 657.

24. William Cullen Bryant, *Letters of a Traveller; Or, Notes of Things Seen in Europe and America* (New York: G. P. Putnam and Co., 1850), 302.

25. For a general discussion of Bryant's views on nature and national identity, see Nash, *Wilderness,* 74–75.

26. Widder, *Mackinac National Park,* 34. Also, see the address list of cottage owners in Kelton, *Annals,* 159, 160.

27. For an uncritical history of the hotel, see John McCabe, *Grand Hotel: Mackinac Island* (Sault Ste. Marie: Unicorn Press, 1987).

28. Havighurst, *Three Flags,* 188.

29. U.S. House, Conger, 2242.

30. U.S. Senate, *Annual Report of Superintendent of Mackinac National Park, 1893,* letter from Assistant Secretary of War L. A. Grant, 52d Cong., 2d sess., 1893, Ex. Doc 28, microfiche, 3.

31. Widder, *Mackinac National Park,* 17.

32. U.S. Senate, *Sale of Military Reservation on Island of Bois Blanc, in Straits of Mackinaw, Mich.,* 48th Cong., 1st sess., 1884, S. Rept. 378, microfiche, 1.

33. U.S. Senate, *The Condition of Mackinac National Park,* letter from Assistant Secretary of War L. A. Grant, 52d Cong., 2d sess., 1892, Ex. Doc. 21, microfiche, 2.

34. U.S. Senate, *Annual Report of Superintendant, 1893,* 2.

35. Widder, *Reveille Till Taps,* 56.

36. Widder, *Mackinac National Park,* 13.

37. Ibid., 11–12.

38. U.S. Senate, *Annual Report of Superintendant, 1893,* 2.

39. Allen R. Millett and Peter Maslowski, *For the Common Defense: A Military History of the United States of America* (New York: Free Press, 1984), 241.

40. Widder, *Mackinac National Park,* 42.

41. Ibid., 43.

42. Michigan Senate, A Motion to Oppose the Repeal of The Act Setting Aside Certain Lands on the Island of Mackinac as a National Park, *Journal of the Senate* (4 February 1895), 1:211.

43. Michigan Senate, A Resolution Requesting that Our Senators and Representatives in Congress Use All Honorable Means to Cause the United States Government to Cede to the State of Michigan the Island of Mackinac, *Journal of the Senate* (13 February 1895), 1:276; and *Mackinac Island State Park Act,* in Wood, *Historic Mackinac,* 488.

44. Widder, *Mackinac National Park,* 46.

45. Havighurst, *Three Flags,* 195.

46. U.S. House, Conger, 2242.

CHAPTER 4

1. U.S. House, Representative Vandever of California speaking for the Resolution to Set Aside Lands Including the Fresno-Tulare Grove, *Congressional Record* 51st Cong., 1st sess.,(23 August 1890), 21, pt. 9:9072.

2. U.S. Senate, Senator Plumb of Kansas speaking for the Resolution to Set Apart a Certain Tract of Land in the State of California as a Forest Reservation, *Congressional Record* 51st Cong., 1st sess.,(30 September 1890), 21, pt. 11:10740.

3. H. Duane Hampton, *How the U.S. Cavalry Saved Our National Parks* (Bloomington: Indiana University Press, 1971), 143.

4. Mark Spence, "Dispossessing the Wilderness: Yosemite Indians and the National Park Ideal, 1864–1930," *Pacific Historical Review* 65 (February 1996): 30–31; and Alfred Runte, *Yosemite: The Embattled Wilderness* (Lincoln: University of Nebraska Press, 1990), 8–12.

5. Runte, *Embattled Wilderness,* 12.

6. Richard H. Dillon, "The Most Unique and Majestic of Nature's Marvels," *American History Illustrated* 25 (September/October 1990): 59.

7. Hampton, *U.S. Cavalry*, 131.

8. Anne Whiston Spirn, "Constructing Nature: The Legacy of Frederick Law Olmsted," in *Uncommon Ground*, 91–92.

9. Ibid., 92–95.

10. Katherine Ames Taylor, *Yosemite: Trails and Tales* (Stanford, Calif.: Stanford University Press, 1948), 12.

11. Hampton, *U.S. Cavalry*, 138–40.

12. John Muir, *Our National Parks* (Boston: Houghton, Mifflin, and Company, 1902), 318; and Hampton, *U.S. Cavalry*, 138.

13. John Ise, *Our National Park Policy* (Baltimore: Johns Hopkins University Press, 1961), 56.

14. U.S. House, *Annual Report of Acting Superintendent of Yosemite National Park, 1891*, 52d Cong., 1st sess., 1891, Ex. Doc. 1, microfiche, 659.

15. Ibid., 361.

16. Taylor, *Trails and Tales*, 12.

17. Linda Wedel Greene, *Yosemite: The Park and Its Resources* (Washington, D.C.: National Park Service, 1987), 2:373.

18. Ibid., 2:361.

19. Runte, *Embattled Wilderness*, 73–80.

20. Ibid., 58.

21. According to Polly Welts Kaufman, this rugged, military image for rangers undermined the reputation of naturalists and other educators in the Park Service. In an attempt to shed the naturalists' image as effeminate "pansy pickers," the Park Service, which had employed a few female naturalists after 1915, stopped hiring women in the 1930s. The Park Service began to hire women again in the 1960s to serve as interpreters and guides at national historic sites. Women were believed to be well suited for these positions, because supposedly they had good social skills and could handle repetitive jobs better than men. See *National Parks and the Woman's Voice: A History* (Albuquerque: University of New Mexico Press, 1996), 86–87, 121–26.

22. Paul Herman Buck, *The Evolution of the National Park System of the United States* (Washington, D.C.: Government Printing Office, 1946), 36.

23. Ise, *Park Policy*, 98.

24. U.S. House, *Annual Report of Acting Superintendent of Sequoia National Park, 1891*, 52d Cong., 1st sess., 1891, Ex. Doc. 1, microfiche, 667–68.

25. Ise, *Park Policy*, 98.

26. U.S. House, *Annual Report of Acting Superintendent of Sequoia National Park, 1891*, 673.

27. Hampton, *U.S. Cavalry*, 159.

28. Ibid., 160.

29. Ise, *Park Policy*, 110.

30. House, *Annual Report of Acting Superintendent of Sequoia National Park, 1891*, 669.

31. Greene, *Yosemite*, 2:377.

32. Runte, *Embattled Wilderness*, 59–66. Although a few army men recognized the wisdom of spot-burning, even John Muir was suspicious of the practice. The army developed its management policies through trial and error.

33. Runte, "Changing of the Guard," and "Self-Interest and Environment," in *Embattled Wilderness*, 83–99, 181–200.

34. Spence, "Dispossessing the Wilderness," 35–38.

35. Ibid., 46–56.

36. See Runte, "Management Adrift," in *Embattled Wilderness*, 201–18.

37. U.S. House, *Annual Report of Acting Superintendent of Sequoia National Park, 1891,* 669.

CHAPTER 5

1. Although these parks are examined rarely by historians, John Ise dedicates a short chapter to them ("Three Inferior National Parks: Wind Cave, Sullys Hill, and Platt," in *Our National Park Policy* [Baltimore: Johns Hopkins University Press, 1961], 136–42). Ise argues that these parks "did not measure up" to the other early parks (136). Alfred Runte suggests that these parks were an attempt to give midwesterners and easterners more of a stake in the national park experiment (*National Parks: The American Experience,* 3d ed. [Lincoln: University of Nebraska Press, 1997], 214). Passages from this chapter were published in "Adapting to Endure: The Early History of Wind Cave National Park, 1903–1916," *South Dakota History* 32 (summer 2002): 149–64.

2. National Park Service, *Wind Cave* (Washington, D.C.: U.S. Department of the Interior, 1979), 32.

3. Ibid., 35.

4. Ibid., 35–68.

5. Ibid., 68–69.

6. U.S. House, *Report on the Bill to Set Apart Certain Lands in the State of South Dakota as a Public Park, to be Known as Wind Cave National Park,* 57th Cong., 1st sess., 1902, H.R. 2606, 2.

7. Ibid., 1; Ise, *Park Policy,* 137.

8. Alfred Runte, "'Worthless' Lands—Our National Parks," *American West* 15 (May 1973): 5.

9. Runte, *National Parks,* 50.

10. Crater Lake had only one ranger until 1912. Mount Rainier did not receive any money for a superintendent or staff for seven years. (Ise, *Park Policy,* 121–22, 132.)

11. U.S. Senate, *Report on the Bill to Set Apart Certain Lands in the State of South Dakota as a Public Park, to be Known as Wind Cave National Park,* 57th Cong., 1st sess., 1902, S.R. 1944, 3; U.S. House, *Wind Cave National Park,* 1902, H.R. 2606, 5.

12. U.S. Senate, *Wind Cave National Park,* 1902, S.R. 1944, 2.

13. U.S. House, Representative Lacey speaking for the Resolution to Set Apart Certain Lands in the State of South Dakota to be known as the Wind Cave National Park, 57th Cong., 2d sess., *Congressional Record* (6 December 1902), 81.

14. John W. Bohi, "Seventy-Five Years at Wind Cave: A History of the National Park," *South Dakota Historical Collections* 31 (1962): 430; and Ise, *Park Policy,* 139.

15. Harlean James, *Romance of the National Parks* (New York: Macmillan Company, 1939), 67; and Robert Sterling Yard, *The Book of the National Parks* (New York: Charles Scribner's Sons, 1919), 415. See also Ronald Foresta, *National Parks and Their Keepers* (Washington, D.C.: Resources for the Future, Inc., 1984), 11; *National Parks for a New Generation: Visions, Realities, Prospects* (Washington, D.C.: Conservation Foundation, 1985), 36; and Robert Sterling Yard, *Our Federal Lands: A Romance of American Development* (New York: Charles Scribner's Sons, 1928), 248.

16. Ise, *Park Policy,* 159.

17. Yard, *Federal Lands,* 275.

18. Foresta, *Parks and Their Keepers,* 12.

19. H. Duane Hampton, *How the U.S. Cavalry Saved Our National Parks* (Bloomington: Indiana University Press, 1971), 160.

20. Paul Herman Buck, *The Evolution of the National Park System of the United States* (Washington, D.C.: Government Printing Office, 1946), 11.

21. U.S. House, *Report of the Acting Superintendent of the Wind Cave National Park,* Letter from Frederic N. Dille, Acting Superintendent, 63d Cong., 3d sess., 1914, H. Doc. 1475, 873.

22. U.S. House, *Report on Wind Cave National Park, Sullys Hill Park, Casa Grand Ruin, Muir Woods, Petrified Forest, and Other National Monuments,* 63d Cong., 2d sess., 1913, H. Doc. 1009, 359.

23. Bohi, "Seventy-Five Years at Wind Cave," 422–23, and U.S. House, *Report on Glacier and Other Parks and Monuments,* 61st Cong., 3d sess., 1910, H. Doc. 1006, 557.

24. U.S. House, *Report of the Acting Superintendent,* 1914, H. Doc. 1475, 872.

25. National Park Service, *Wind Cave.* See also Devereux Butcher, *Exploring Our National Parks and Monuments* (Boston: Houghton Mifflin Company, 1967), 159–63; O. W. Coursey, *Beautiful Black Hills* (Mitchell, S. Dak.: Educator Supply Co., 1926), 179–80; Michael Frome, *National Park Guide* (Chicago: Rand McNally, 1988), 146; Freeman Tilden, *The National Parks* (New York: Alfred A. Knopf, 1986), 241–44; and Dorr G. Yeager, *Your Western National Parks: A Guide* (New York: Dodd, Mead and Co., 1947), 28–31.

26. U.S. House, *Report on Wind Cave National Park,* 1913, H. Doc. 1009, 864.

27. Ise, *Park Policy,* 140.

28. U.S. House, *Report on Sullys Hill Park, Casa Grande Ruin, Muir Woods, Petrified Forest, and Other National Monuments,* 63d Cong., 3d sess., 1914, H. Doc. 1475, 882.

29. U.S. House, *Report on Wind Cave, Crater Lake, Platt, and Sullys Hill National Parks, and Casa Grande Ruin,* 61st Cong., 2d sess., 1909, H. Doc. 107, 515.

30. U.S. House, *Report on Sullys Hill Park,* 1914, H. Doc. 1475, 882.

31. U.S. House, *Report on Platt and Wind Cave National Parks, Sullys Hill Parks, Casa Grande Ruin, Muir Woods, Petrified Forest, and Other National Monuments,* 62d Cong., 3d sess., 1912, H. Doc. 933, 767.

32. U.S. House, *Report on Wind Cave,* 1909, H. Doc. 107, 515.

33. U.S. House, *Report on Sullys Hill Park,* 1914, H. Doc. 1475, 882.

34. U.S. House, *For the Transfer of Jurisdiction over Sullys Hill National Park From the Department of the Interior to the Department of Agriculture, to be Maintained as the Sullys Hill National Game Preserve,* 71st Cong., 2d sess., 1930, H.R. 2014, 3.

35. Ibid.

36. Ibid., 2.

37. Mackinac National Park, which was declassified in 1895, could have been considered a health resort as well as a historic park. Hot Springs, Arkansas, was still a reserve in 1916.

38. Ballard M. Barker and William Carl Jameson, *Platt National Park: Environment and Ecology* (Norman: University of Oklahoma Press, 1975), 22.

39. U.S. House, *Sulfur Springs Reservation to Be Known as Platt National Park,* 59th Cong., 1st sess., 1906, H.R. 5016, 1.

40. U.S. House, *Report on Glacier,* 1910, H. Doc. 1006, 558.

41. Hampton, *U.S. Cavalry,* 160; and Ise, *Park Policy,* 132.

42. Foresta, *Parks and Their Keepers,* 12.

43. U.S. House, *Report on Wind Cave,* 1909, H. Doc. 107, 512.

44. Ibid., 514, and U.S. House, *Report of the Superintendent of the Platt National Park,* Letter from W. J. French, Superintendent, 63d Cong., 2d sess., 1913, H. Doc. 1009, 847.

45. U.S. House, *Report of the Superintendent of the Platt National Park,* Letter from R. A. Sneed, Superintendent, 63d Cong., 3d sess., 1914, H. Doc. 1475, 850.

46. Barker and Jameson, *Platt,* 22.

CHAPTER 6

1. Allen R. Millett and Peter Maslowski, *For the Common Defense: A Military History of the United States of America* (New York: Free Press, 1984), 309.

2. Audrey L. Haines, *The Yellowstone Story: A History of Our First National Park* (Denver: Colorado Associated University Press, 1977), 455.

3. H. Duane Hampton, *How the U.S. Cavalry Saved Our National Parks* (Bloomington: Indiana University Press, 1971), 176.

4. Ibid., 178.

5. Richard White, *"It's Your Misfortune and None of My Own": A New History of the American West* (Norman: University of Oklahoma Press, 1991), 409–12.

6. Ibid.

7. Roderick Nash, *Wilderness and the American Mind* (New Haven, Conn.: Yale University Press. 1967), 161–62, 176.

8. Ibid., 170–81.

9. *An Act to Establish a National Park Service, and for Other Purposes, Statutes at Large,* 39, sec. 1, 535 (1916), in *American's National Park System: The Critical Documents,* ed. Lary M. Dilsaver (Lanham, Md.: Rowman & Littlefield Publishers, Inc., 1994), 46.

10. William C. Everhart, *The National Park Service* (New York: Praeger Publishers, 1972), 3–4, and John Ise, *Our National Park Policy* (Baltimore: Johns Hopkins University Press, 1961), 193–94.

11. Thomas A. Wikle, "Proposals, Abolishments, and Changing Standards for U.S. National Parks," *Historian* 54 (autumn 1991): 54–55.

12. Franklin K. Lane, Washington, to Stephen T. Mather, director of the National Park Service, 13 May 1918, in Dilsaver, *Critical Documents,* 48–52. Although this public letter was sent to Mather from Lane, Mather was probably the original source of these ideas.

13. Alfred Runte, *National Parks: The American Experience,* 3d ed. (Lincoln: University of Nebraska Press, 1997), 219.

14. Dilsaver, *Critical Documents,* 111–12.

15. Ibid., 165–66; and Report of the Advisory Board on Wildlife Management Appointed by Secretary of the Interior Udall, *Wildlife Management in the National Parks,* 3 March 1963, in ibid., 239, 250.

16. John F. Kennedy, Washington, D.C., to the delegates to the First World Conference on National Parks, 23 June 1962, in *First World Conference on National Parks: Proceedings of a Conference Organized by the International Union for Conservation of Nature and Natural Resources,* ed. Alexander B. Adams (Washington, D.C.: Department of the Interior, 1962), v.

17. For example, see Jane Pyle's discussion of the International Union for the Conservation of Nature and Natural Resources' recommendations for national parks (1969), from "The Selection of National Parks and Equivalent Reserves in Latin America," in *Papers in Latin American Geography in Honor of Lucia C. Harrison,* ed. Oscar H. Horst (Muncie, Ind.: Conference of Latin American Geographers, 1981), 57–58. See also John Shultis, "Improving the Wilderness: Common Factors in Creating National Parks and Equivalent Reserves during the Nineteenth Century," *Forest and Conservation History* 39 (July 1995): 121–27.

18. Joseph L. Sax, *Mountains without Handrails: Reflections on the National Parks* (Ann Arbor: University of Michigan Press, 1980): 103–13.

19. Dwight F. Rettie, *Our National Park System: Caring for America's Greatest Natural and Historic Treasures* (Urbana: University of Illinois Press, 1995), 73–85.

20. Dilsaver, *Critical Documents,* 371.

BIBLIOGRAPHY

SECONDARY SOURCES—GENERAL

Albright, Horace M. *Origins of National Park Service Administration of Historic Sites.* Philadelphia: Eastern National Park and Monument Association, 1971.

Albright, Horace M., and Robert Cahn. *The Birth of the National Park Service: The Founding Years, 1913–33.* Salt Lake City: Howe Brothers, 1985.

Bearss, Edwin C. "The National Park Service and Its History Program: 1864–1986—An Overview." *Public Historian* 9 (spring 1987): 10–18.

Buck, Paul Herman. "The Evolution of the National Park System of the United States." Master's thesis, The Ohio State University, 1922.

———. *The Evolution of the National Park System of the United States.* Washington, D.C.: Government Printing Office, 1946.

Butcher, Devereux. *Exploring Our National Parks and Monuments.* Boston: Houghton Mifflin Company, 1967.

Cronon, William, ed. *Uncommon Ground: Rethinking the Human Place in Nature.* New York: W. W. Norton & Company, 1996.

Dulles, Foster Rhea. *A History of Recreation: America Learns to Play.* New York: Meredith Publishing Company, 1965.

Everhart, William C. *The National Park Service.* New York: Praeger Publishers, 1972.

Foresta, Ronald A. *America's National Parks and Their Keepers.* Washington, D.C.: Resources for the Future, 1984.

Frome, Michael. *Back Then: A Pictorial History of America's National Parks.* Minocqua, Wis.: NorthWord Press, 1990.

———. *National Park Guide.* Chicago: Rand McNally, 1988.

Hampton, H. Duane. *How the U.S. Cavalry Saved Our National Parks.* Bloomington: Indiana University Press, 1971.

———. "Opposition to National Parks." *Journal of Forest History* 25 (January 1981): 37–45.

Harrison, Robert Pogue. *Forests: The Shadow of Civilization.* Chicago: University of Chicago Press, 1992.

Horst, Oscar H., ed. *Papers in Latin American Geography in Honor of Lucia C. Harrison.* Muncie, Ind.: Conference of Latin American Geographers, 1981.

Hummel, Don. *Stealing the National Parks: The Destruction of Concessions and Park Access.* Bellevue, Wash.: Free Enterprise Press, 1987.

Ise, John. *Our National Park Policy: A Critical History.* Baltimore: Johns Hopkins Press, 1961.

James, Harlean. *Romance of the National Parks.* New York: MacMillan Company, 1939.

Johnson, Jenny Marie, ed. *Exploration and Mapping of the National Parks.* Winnetka, Ill.: Speculum Orbis Press, 1994.

Kaufman, Polly Welts. *National Parks and the Woman's Voice: A History.* Albuquerque: University of New Mexico Press, 1996.

Lee, Ronald F. *The Antiquities Act of 1906.* Washington, D.C.: National Park Service, 1970.

———. *Family Tree of the National Park System.* Philadelphia: Eastern National Park and Monument Association, 1974.

Lewis, John. "A Park System for Everyone." *National Parks* 65 (September 1991): 22–23.

Limerick, Patricia Nelson. *The Legacy of Conquest: The Unbroken Past of the American West.* New York: W. W. Norton and Company, 1987.

Mackintosh, Barry. *The National Parks: Shaping the System.* Washington, D.C.: Department of the Interior, 1991.

Mason, Kathy S. "A Labor of Love and Duty: The U.S. Army and the First Five National Parks." Master's thesis, The Ohio State University, 1994.

———. "Before the Park Service: Standards and Management in the U.S. National Parks, 1872–1916." Ph.D. diss., Miami University, 1999.

Melbo, Irving R. *Our Country's National Parks.* Vol. 1–2. Indianapolis: Bobbs-Merrill Company, 1941.

Meyerson, Harvey. *Nature's Army: When Soldiers Fought for Yosemite.* Lawrence: University Press of Kansas, 2001.

Miles, John C. *Guardians of the Parks: A History of the National Parks and Conservation Association.* Washington, D.C.: Taylor and Francis, 1995.

Millet, Allen R., and Peter Maslowski. *For the Common Defense: A Military History of the United States of America.* New York: Free Press, 1984.

Mogren, Paul Andrew. "The Development of a Philosophy of Land Reservation of General Land Office, United States Forest Service, and National Park Service Land, 1787 to 1947." Ph.D. diss., University of Utah, 1980.

Nash, Roderick. *Wilderness and the American Mind.* New Haven, Conn.: Yale University Press, 1967.

National Parks for a New Generation: Visions, Realities, Prospects. Washington, D.C.: Conservation Foundation, 1985.

Norwood, Vera. *Made from This Earth: American Women and Nature.* Chapel Hill: University of North Carolina Press, 1993.

Pomeroy, Earl. *In Search of the Golden West: The Tourist in Western America.* New York: Alfred A. Knopf, 1957.

Reiger, John F. *American Sportsmen and the Origins of Conservation.* Rev. ed. Norman: University of Oklahoma Press, 1986.

Rettie, Dwight F. *Our National Park System: Caring for America's Greatest Natural and His-*

toric Treasures. Urbana: University of Illinois Press, 1995.

Runte, Alfred. *National Parks: The American Experience*. 3d ed. Lincoln: University of Nebraska Press, 1997.

———. "Preservation Heritage: The Origins of the Park Idea in the United States." In *Indiana Historical Society Lectures, 1983: Perceptions of the Landscape and Its Preservation*. Indianapolis: Indiana Historical Society, 1984.

———. *Public Lands, Public Heritage: The National Forest Idea*. Niwot, Colo.: Roberts Rinehart Publishers, 1991.

———. "'Worthless' Lands—Our National Parks." *American West* 15 (May 1973): 4–11.

Sax, Joseph L. *Mountains without Handrails: Reflections on the National Parks*. Ann Arbor: University of Michigan Press, 1980.

Schene, Michael G. "The National Park Service and Historic Preservation: An Introduction." *Public Historian* 9 (spring 1987): 6–9.

Sellars, Richard W., and Alfred Runte. "The National Parks: A Forum on the 'Worthless Lands' Thesis." *Journal of Forest History* 27 (July 1983): 130–41.

Shultis, John. "Improving the Wilderness: Common Factors in Creating National Parks and Equivalent Reserves during the Nineteenth Century." *Forest and Conservation History* 39 (July 1995): 121–29.

Stevens, Joseph E. *America's National Battlefield Parks: A Guide*. Norman: University of Oklahoma Press, 1990.

Tilden, Freeman. *The National Parks: What They Mean to You and Me*. New York: Alfred A. Knopf, 1955.

Tilden, Freeman, and Paul Schullery. *The National Parks*. New York: Alfred A. Knopf, 1986.

White, Richard. *"It's Your Misfortune and None of My Own": A New History of the American West*. Norman: University of Oklahoma Press, 1991.

Wikle, Thomas A. "Proposals, Abolishments, and Changing Standards for the U.S. National Parks." *Historian* 54 (autumn 1991): 49–64.

Wright, R. Gerald. *National Parks and Protected Areas: Their Role in Environmental Protection*. Cambridge, Mass.: Blackwell Science, 1996.

———. *Wildlife Research and Management in the National Parks*. Urbana: University of Illinois Press, 1992.

Yard, Robert Sterling. *The Book of the National Parks*. New York: Charles Scribner's Sons, 1919.

———. *Glimpses of Our National Parks*. Washington, D.C.: U.S. Department of the Interior, 1931.

———. *The National Parks Portfolio*. Washington, D.C.: U.S. Department of the Interior, 1928.

———. *Our Federal Lands: A Romance of American Development*. New York: Charles Scribner's Sons, 1928.

Yeager, Dorr G. *Your Western National Parks: A Guide*. New York: Dodd, Mead and Co., 1947.

Zaslowsky, Dyan. *These American Lands: Parks, Wilderness, and the Public Lands*. New York: Henry Holt and Company, 1986.

SECONDARY SOURCES—INDIVIDUAL PARKS

Hot Springs

Abbott, Shirley. "Hot Springs, Ark., Fondly Recalled as a Paradise Lost." *Smithsonian* 22 (July 1991): 104–15.

Bedinger, M. S. *Valley of the Vapors: Hot Springs National Park.* Philadelphia: Eastern National Park and Monument Association, 1974.

Danielson, Kay. "Hot Springs Revival." *National Parks* 62 (September/October 1988): 32–35.

Fields, Wayne. "The Double Life of Hot Springs." *American Heritage* 42 (April 1991): 107–15.

Hudgins, Mary D. *A Thumbnail History of Hot Springs.* Hot Springs, Ark.: Hot Springs Natural History Association, 1937.

Hudson, Patricia L. "Taking the Waters in Style." *Americana* 18 (January/February 1991): 42–47.

Miller, George Oxford. "The Valley of the Vapors." *Saturday Evening Post* (January/February 1992): 82–85.

Morgan, James. "Time Out for Bubbles." *Travel and Leisure* 20 (March 1990): 194–96, 206.

Paige, John C., and Laura Soulliere Harrison. *Out of the Vapors: A Social and Architectural History of Bathhouse Row: Hot Springs National Park, Arkansas.* Washington, D.C.: U.S. Department of the Interior, 1988.

Seslar, Patrick. "Hot Springs Arkansas." *Trailer Life* 52 (June 1992): 28–32.

Walls, Edwina. "The Public Health Service VD Clinic in Hot Springs, AR." *Public Health Reports* 110 (January–February 1995): 103–4.

Mackinac

Bowen, Dana Thomas. *Memories of the Lakes: Told in Story and Picture.* Cleveland: Freshwater Press, 1946.

———. *Shipwrecks of the Lakes.* Cleveland: Lakeside Printing Company, 1953.

Feltner, Charles E., and Jeri Baron Feltner. *Shipwrecks of the Straits of Mackinac.* Dearborn, Mich.: Seajay Publications, 1991.

Havighurst, Walter. *Three Flags at the Straits: The Forts of Mackinac.* Englewood Cliffs, N.J.: Prentice-Hall, 1966.

MacCabe, John. *Grand Hotel: Mackinac Island.* Sault Ste. Marie, Mich.: Unicorn Press, 1987.

Mason, Kathy S. "Gem of the Straits: Mackinac 1875–1895." *Inland Seas* 49 (winter 1993): 246–58.

Michigan Biographies. Lansing: Michigan Historical Commission, 1924.

Widder, Keith R. *Mackinac National Park: 1875–1895.* Williamston, Mich.: TriKraft, 1975.

———. *Reveille Till Taps: Soldier Life at Fort Mackinac, 1780–1895.* Williamston, Mich.: TriKraft, 1972.

Sequoia

Dilsaver, Lary M., and William C. Tweed. *Challenge of the Big Trees of Sequoia and Kings Canyon National Parks.* Three Rivers, Calif.: Sequoia Natural History Association, 1990.

Howells, Bob. "Happy Birthday, Yosemite and Sequoia." *Trailer Life* 50 (September 1990): 50–54.

National Park Service. *Sequoia and Kings Canyon: A Guide to Sequoia and Kings Canyon National Parks.* Washington, D.C.: U.S. Department of the Interior, 1992.

"Superlatives." *Life* 14 (summer 1991): 98–110.

Yellowstone

Barber, John F. *Old Yellowstone Views.* Missoula, Mont.: Mountain Press Publishing Company, 1987.

Beard, Frances Birkhead, ed. *Wyoming: From Territorial Days to the Present.* Vol. 1, *Yellowstone Park and Transportation Problems.* Chicago: American Historical Society, 1933.

Byrand, Sherri. "Grace under Pressure." *National Parks* 71 (March 1997): 27–29.

Chablin, Thomas S., ed. *The Historical Encyclopedia of Wyoming.* Cheyenne: Wyoming Historical Institute, 1970. S.v. "Yellowstone National Park."

Chittenden, Hiram Martin. *The Yellowstone National Park: Historical and Descriptive.* 4th ed. Cincinnati: Robert Clarke Company, 1933.

Early, Katherine E. *"For the Benefit and Enjoyment of the People:" Cultural Attitudes and the Establishment of Yellowstone National Park.* Washington, D.C.: Georgetown University Press, 1984.

Haines, Aubrey L. *Yellowstone National Park: Its Exploration and Establishment.* Washington, D.C.: National Park Service, 1974.

———. *The Yellowstone Story: A History of Our First National Park.* Vol. 1–2. Denver: Colorado Associated University Press, 1977.

Hutton, Paul A. "Phil Sheridan's Crusade for Yellowstone." *American History Illustrated* 19 (February 1985): 7, 11–15.

Schullery, Paul. "Before the Park: Yellowstone through the Millennia." *Orion* 16 (spring 1997): 24–26.

White, Stuart Sherman. "The National Parks—100 Years Later: A Photojournalist's Study of the Changing Philosophy of the National Parks System, Observed and Photographed in Yellowstone." Master's thesis, Kent State University, 1973.

Yosemite

Dillon, Richard H. "The Most Unique and Majestic of Nature's Marvels." *American History Illustrated* 25 (September–October 1990): 54–67.

Greene, Linda Wedel. *Yosemite: The Park and its Resources.* Vol. 1–3. Washington, D.C.: National Park Service, 1991.

Meyerson, Harvey. *Nature's Army: When Soldiers Fought for Yosemite.* Lawrence: University Press of Kansas, 2001.

Orsi, Richard J., Alfred Runte, and Marlene Smith-Baranzini, eds. *Yosemite and Sequoia: A Century of California National Parks.* Berkeley: University of California Press, 1993.

Runte, Alfred. *Yosemite: The Embattled Wilderness.* Lincoln: University of Nebraska Press, 1990.

Spence, Mark. "Dispossessing the Wilderness: Yosemite Indians and the National Park Ideal, 1864–1930." *Pacific Historical Review* 65 (February 1996): 27–59.

Taylor, Katherine Ames. *Yosemite: Trails and Tales*. Stanford, Calif.: Stanford University Press, 1948.

Wind Cave and Sully's Hill

Bohi, John W. "Seventy-Five Years at Wind Cave: A History of the National Park." *South Dakota Historical Collections* 31 (1962): 365–468.

Casey, Robert J. *The Black Hills and Their Incredible Characters: A Chronicle and a Guide*. Indianapolis: Bobbs-Merrill Company, 1949.

Coursey, O. W. *Beautiful Black Hills*. Mitchell, S.D.: Educator Supply Company, 1926.

La Pierre, Yvette. "A Place to Park." *Home and Away* 16 (March/April 1995): 14–19.

Mason, Kathy S. "Adapting to Endure: The Early History of Wind Cave National Park, 1903–1916." *South Dakota History* 32 (summer 2002): 149–64.

National Park Service. *Wind Cave*. Washington, D.C.: U.S. Department of the Interior, 1979.

Reese, Lisle M. *South Dakota: A Guide to the State*. New York: Hastings House, 1952.

Shore, Debra. "While You're Out There . . . Eight Unsung Parks also Worth a Visit." *Outside* 17 (June 1992): 85.

Shute, Nancy. "National Parks." *Travel and Leisure* 23 (June 1993): 92–99.

Others

"All's Quiet at Lassen." *Sunset* 183 (August 1989): 16–21.

Barker, Ballard M., and William Carl Jameson. *Platt National Park: Environment and Ecology*. Norman: University of Oklahoma Press, 1975.

Boorstein, Margaret. "The Wonders and Origins of Four National Parks of the Southern United States." *Focus* 42 (winter 1992): 26–31.

Smith, Duane A. *Mesa Verde National Park: Shadows of the Centuries*. Lawrence: University Press of Kansas, 1988.

Stringham, Emerson. *Mesa Verde National Park*. Madison, Wis.: Pacot Publications, 1946.

"Wilderness." *National Parks* 63 (July 1989): 39–41.

Williams, John H. *The Mountain that was "God": Being a Little Book About the Great Peak Which the Indians Named "Tacoma" but Which is Officially Called "Rainier."* New York: G. P. Putnam's Sons, 1911.

PRIMARY SOURCES

Hot Springs

Allen, L. M. *Hot Springs National Park, Arkansas*. Hot Springs, Ark.: Rock Island Lines, 1922.

Department of the Interior. *General Information Regarding the Hot Springs of Arkansas*. Washington, D.C.: Government Printing Office, 1912.

Fordyce Bath House: Arkansas Hot Springs. Hot Springs, Ark.: Privately printed, n.d.

Legend of the Quapaw Baths. Reprint, Hot Springs, Ark.: Eastern National Park Association, 1984.

National Park Service. *Hot Springs.* Washington, D.C.: Government Printing Office, 1994.

Report of the Superintendent of the Hot Springs Reservation. Washington, D.C.: Government Printing Office, 1899.

Mackinac Island

Bailey, John R. *Mackinac, Formerly Michilimackinac: A History and Guide Book with Maps.* Grand Rapids, Mich.: Tradesman Company, 1895.

Baird, Elizabeth Therese. "Reminiscences of Early Days on Mackinac Island." In *Collections of the State Historical Society of Wisconsin,* 14:17–64. Madison, Wis.: Democrat Printing Company, 1898.

Bingham, Angie. "Devil's Kitchen, Mackinac Island." In *Collections and Researches Made by the Michigan Pioneer and Historical Society,* 29:336–37. Lansing, Mich.: Wynkoop, Hallenbeck, Crawford Company, 1901.

Bryant, William Cullen. *Letters of a Traveller; or, Notes of Things Seen in Europe and America.* New York: G. P. Putman and Company, 1850.

Disturnell, John. *The Great Lakes, or Inland Seas of America.* New York: American News Company, 1868.

Ferry, Thomas W. "The Growth and Progress of Michigan." Paper read at the Annual Meeting of the Pioneer Society of Michigan, 8 June 1882. In *Report of the Pioneer Society of the State of Michigan,* 5:21–26. Lansing, Mich.: W. S. George and Company, 1884.

Henry, Alexander. *Attack at Michilimackinac: Alexander Henry's Travels and Adventures in Canada and the Indian Territories between the Years 1760 and 1764.* Edited by David A. Armour. Lansing, Mich.: TriKraft, 1971.

Heydenburk, Martin. "Mackinaw Re-visited—How it Looked Forty Years Ago—Petoskey and the Camp-meeting." In *Report of the Pioneer Society of the State of Michigan,* 7:196–98. Lansing, Mich.: Thorp and Godfrey, 1886.

"The Island of Mackinac." In *Historical Collections of the Michigan Pioneer and Historical Society,* 28:641–95. Lansing, Mich.: Robert Smith and Company, 1892. First published in the *Detroit Free Press.*

Kelton, Dwight. *Annals of Fort Mackinac.* Detroit: Detroit Free Press Printing Co., 1894.

"Mackinac." In *Report of the Pioneer Society of the State of Michigan,* 7:198–202. Lansing, Mich.: Thorp and Godfrey, 1886. First published in the *New York Tribune,* 1859.

"A Mackinac Pioneer." In *Report of the Pioneer Society of the State of Michigan,* 7:198. Lansing, Mich.: Thorp and Godfrey, 1886. First published in the *Detroit Post and Tribune,* 14 June 1884.

Michigan Historical Commission. *Bulletin No. 5: Names of Places of Interest on Mackinac Island, Michigan, Established, Designated, and Adopted by the Mackinac Island State Park Commission and the Michigan Historical Commission.* Lansing, Mich.: Wynkoop, Hallenbeck, Crawford Co., 1916.

Michigan Senate. *Journal of the Senate.* 1895.

Schoolcraft, Henry R. *Personal Memoir of a Residence of Thirty Years with the Indian Tribes on the American Frontiers.* Philadelphia: Lippincott, Gramo, and Co., 1851.

Strickland, W. P. *Old Mackinaw: or the Fortress of the Lakes and its Surroundings.* Philadelphia: James Challen and Son, 1860.

Van Fleet, J. A. *Old and New Mackinac: With Copious Extracts from Marquette, Hennepin, La Hontan, Alexander Henry, and Others.* Grand Rapids, Mich.: "The Lever" Book and Job Office, 1880.

Williams, Meade C. *Early Mackinac: A Sketch, Historical and Descriptive.* St. Louis: Buchart Brothers, 1897.

Wood, Edwin Orin. *Historic Mackinac: The Historical, Picturesque and Legendary Features of the Mackinac Country.* New York: Macmillan Company, 1918.

Yellowstone

Campbell, Reau. *Complete Guide and Descriptive Book of the Yellowstone Park.* Chicago: Rogers and Smith Co., 1909.

Everts, T. C. "Thirty-seven Days of Peril." In *Contributions to the Historical Society of Montana,* 5:395–427. Boston: J. S. Canner and Company, 1966. First published in *Scribner's Magazine,* November 1871.

Folsom, David E. "The Folsom-Cook Exploration of the Upper Yellowstone in the Year 1869." In *Contributions to the Historical Society of Montana,* 5:349–69. Boston: J. S. Canner and Company, 1966.

Gerrish, Theodore. *Life in the World's Wonderland, Illustrated: A Graphic Description of the Great Northwest, From St. Paul, Minnesota, to the Land of the Midnight Sun.* Biddeford, Maine: Biddeford Journal, 1887.

Hedges, Cornelius. "Journal of Judge Cornelius Hedges." In *Contributions to the Historical Society of Montana,* 5:370–94. Boston: J. S. Canner and Company, 1966.

Kipling, Rudyard. *American Notes.* Boston: Brown and Company, 1899.

Langford, Nathaniel Pitt. *Diary of the Washburn Expedition to the Yellowstone and Firehole River in the Year 1870.* St. Paul, Minn.: F. J. Haynes Company, 1905.

Quivey, Addison M. "The Yellowstone Expedition of 1874." In *Contributions to the Historical Society of Montana,* 1:149–233. Boston: J. S. Canner and Company, 1966.

Richardson, James. *Wonders of the Yellowstone.* New York: Charles Scribner's Sons, 1886.

Riley, W. C. *Official Guide to the Yellowstone National Park: A Manual for Tourists.* St. Paul, Minn.: Northern News Co., 1888.

Roberts, Edwards. *Shoshone and Other Western Wonders.* New York: Harper and Brothers, 1888.

Wylie, W. W. *Yellowstone National Park; or the Great American Wonderland: A Complete Hand or Guide Book for Tourists.* Kansas City, Mo.: Ramsey, Millet and Hudson, 1882.

Yosemite

Beadle, J. H. "By Horseback into Yosemite, 1871." *American History Illustrated* 25 (September–October 1990): 61.

"Early Days in Yosemite—A Trip to the Yosemite Falls." *California Historical Society Quarterly* 1 (January 1923): 274–83. First published in *Mariposa Democrat,* 5 August 1856.

Muir, John. *My First Summer in the Sierra.* With an Introduction by Gretel Ehrlich. New York: Penguin Books, 1987.

Russell, Carl P. "Early Years in Yosemite." *California Historical Society Quarterly* 5 (December 1926): 328–41.

Taylor, F. J. *The Yosemite Trip Book.* San Francisco: H. S. Crocker Company, 1927.

Other Primary Sources

Adams, Alexander B., ed. *First World Conference on National Parks: Proceedings of a Conference Organized by the International Union for Conservation of Nature and Natural Resources.* Washington, D.C.: Department of the Interior, 1962.

Annual reports of the superintendents of the parks.

Congressional Globe. 46 vols. Washington, D.C., 1834–73.

Congressional Record.

Dilsaver, Lary M., ed. *America's National Park System: The Critical Documents.* Lanham, Md.: Rowman and Littlefield, 1994.

Executive documents pertaining to individual national parks.

General Information Regarding Crater Lake National Park: Season of 1914. Washington, D.C.: Government Printing Office, 1914.

House and Senate documents pertaining to individual national parks.

Muir, John. *Our National Parks.* Boston: Houghton, Mifflin, and Company, 1902.

Murphy, Thomas Dowler. *Seven Wonderlands of the American West; Being the Notes of a Traveler Concerning Various Pilgrimages to the Yellowstone National Park, the Yosemite National Park, the Grand Canyon National Park, Zion National Park, Glacier National Park, Crater Lake National Park and the Petrified Forests of Arizona.* Boston: L. C. Page and Company, 1925.

National Park Service. *General Information Regarding the National Monuments.* Washington, D.C.: Government Printing Office, 1917.

———. *The National Parks: Lesser-known Areas.* Washington, D.C.: U.S. Department of the Interior, 1995.

Proceedings of the National Park Conference Held at the Yellowstone National Park, September 11 and 12, 1911. Washington, D.C.: Government Printing Office, 1912.

War Department. *National Military Park, National Park, Battlefield Site, and National Monument Regulations.* Washington, D.C.: U.S. Government Printing Office, 1931.

INDEX

Michigan State University Press is committed to preserving ancient forests and antural resources. We have elected to print this title on New Leaf EcoOffset 100, which is 100% recycled (100% post-consumer waste) and processed chlorine free (PCF). As a result of our paper choice, Michigan State University Press has saved the following natural resources*:

7	Trees (40 feet in height)
336	Pounds of Solid Waste
3,016	Gallons of Water
5	Million BTUs of Energy
663	Pounds of Greenhouse Gases
2	Pounds of Air Emissions (HAPs, VOCs, TRSs combined)
21	Pounds of Hazardous Effluent (BODs, TSSs, CODs, and AOXs combined)

We are a member of Green Press Initiative—a nonprofit program dedicated to supporting book publishers in maximizing their use of fiber that is not sourced from ancient or endangered forests. For more information about Green Press Initiative and the use of recycled paper in book publishing, please visit *www.greenpressinitiative.org*.

*Environmental benefits are calculated by New Leaf Paper based on research done by the Environmental Defense Fund and other members of the Paper Task Force who study the environmental impacts of the paper industry.